Praise for
PASSING *for* NORMAL

"A compulsive telling . . . that the diagnosis should come so late and that an intelligent family and friends should be so uninformed suggest the need for books like Wilensky's."

—*Kirkus Reviews*

"Wilensky's account is an intriguing mixture of hiding, acceptance, and perceptive observation. She deals unflinchingly with the impact of her conditions on her relationships with fellow students, teachers, and family members."

—*Booklist*

"[*Passing for Normal*] is a moving blend of wiseguy humor and (predictably) detailed weirdness."

—*New York Daily News*

"The tale of the way Wilensky denied her problem and 'passed,' and the emotional toll such effort took, has a happy ending . . . The result is not a fairy-tale success story but a real one."

—*Entertainment Weekly*

PASSING *for* NORMAL

a memoir of compulsion

AMY S. WILENSKY

BROADWAY BOOKS / NEW YORK

BROADWAY

A hardcover edition of this book was published in 1999 by
Broadway Books.

Visit our website at www.broadwaybooks.com

First trade paperback edition published 2000.

The Library of Congress has cataloged the hardcover edition as:
Wilensky, Amy S., 1969–
Passing for normal: a memoir of compulsion /
by Amy S. Wilensky.
p.   cm.
1. Wilensky, Amy S., 1969– . 2. Obsessive-compulsive
disorder—Patients Biography. 3. Tourette syndrome—
Patients Biography.
I. Title.
RC533.W54A3   1999   99-24312
CIP

ISBN 0-7679-0186-X

146122990

For Papa, like I always promised

There is an optical illusion about every person we meet. In truth, they are all creatures of a given temperament, which will appear in a given character, whose boundaries they will never pass: but we look at them, they seem alive, and we presume there is impulse in them. In the moment it seems impulse; in the year, in the lifetime, it turns out to be a certain uniform tune which the revolving barrel of the music-box must play.

—RALPH WALDO EMERSON, from "Experience"

ACKNOWLEDGMENTS

I am honored to be writing under the guidance of my agent, the superlative Amanda Urban, who is a vibrant and inspiring force; her assistant at ICM, Jenna Lamond, has also been tremendously helpful throughout the process of putting it all together. My editor at Broadway Books, Charlie Conrad, has understood this project from day one, perhaps better than I have, and without his sharp eye and unwavering support, I never would have had the courage to begin, let alone finish it; working with him is a real pleasure. I would like to offer my most sincere gratitude to the supremely gifted Becky Cole, also at Broadway, without whom I am no longer certain I could write a book, and the infinitely patient Ted Sammons, formerly at Broadway, who so gracefully pulled me through the roughest patch; I hope he is happy and well.

I would like to thank Dr. Ira Feirstein and Dr. Jill Poller for their professional wisdom and capacity for compassion, as well as all those who are researching, writing about, and talking about Tourette's and OCD; rest assured, your efforts are not going unnoticed by those who need them most.

ACKNOWLEDGMENTS

At Columbia University, Richard Locke is proving that there are still people out there who treasure the written word. He has been a mentor to me in the truest sense, and I feel fortunate for having been able to learn from him. I owe so much to so many teachers, but William Gifford and Le Anne Schreiber, in particular, have always understood implicitly. To these three wise voices, who set the bar higher and then higher still, you give me something to strive for.

It goes without saying that I have the best friends in the world, but without Bryant Palmer, I would probably be in a locked ward somewhere; in case he doesn't know, I consider this story as much his as mine, and I give thanks for him every day of my life. I owe more than I can ever say to my best reader, Caroline Suh, who keeps me honest and makes me proud, and to Nicole Laborde, who has taught me much of what I know about friendship. Ben, I love you always: You make everything better.

Most of all, I would like to thank my family, all of them, of course, but especially Ellen Dorothy Borg and Alison, Sandra, and Joel Wilensky. Mormor, your faith in me is sustaining. Ali, I want you to know how much I try to be like you, in all the best possible ways. And Mom and Dad: Yes, it's true. I hold you responsible for everything. All I am, I am because of you.

CONTENTS

All I hear is the thwack of the ball on the floor; the voices of the other kids blend into a faint humming buzz that seems to get farther and farther away. I keep dribbling, and the bouncing takes on a rhythm, 4/4, which I know from cello lessons and piano lessons and recorder lessons and even know how to conduct, which I do then in my head as I keep bouncing. The accent is on the first beat, or syllable; the phrase, as I know to call it, is this, drilled into the bows and fingers and windpipes of child musicians everywhere: ONE two three four, ONE two three four, BOUNCE bounce bounce bounce, BOUNCE bounce bounce bounce, each thwack impeccably timed, the ball speeding into the floor and then back before I so much as register its departure, smack into my waiting open palm.

On the horizon I see the gym teacher standing with his hands in the air, see his mouth open wide and then shut in a malformed O. Wait: It's open again; he's yelling something, but it's not to me or I would hear it, I think then, I would hear. Or maybe I can't hear him, have suddenly lost my ability to hear, am having a stroke like my grandfather, my father's father, who died before I was born and whom I always picture in a wheelchair with his head slumped to one side; I realize in the bouncing that I'm not even sure what he looked like standing up, before he was paralyzed: Where did all the prestroke photos go?

Someone elbows me and it all becomes clear: He is talking to me, is telling me to hurry up, take my turn, shoot the ball, so I start to move forward, but the backboard is blurry, like watery paint, and all I can see is the gym teacher, his mouth opening and closing like a far-off fish. Then, just as I get close enough to take a legitimate shot, the bouncing turns into words midthwack like an Escher drawing, with no spot to pinpoint the transformation, and the bounce becomes a syllable, each bounce becomes a word.

This. is. not. me. say the bounces, one word for each bounce, one beat for each word, and I like the sound of the words in my head, the way they match the bounces, and I bounce faster, say the words faster, until the words latch on to each other at the ends and become one long word, with four fast bounce beats: ThisisnotmeThisisnotme.

I may have kept bouncing until I dropped from exhaustion, wore size-2 shoe grooves into the hard scuffed floor of the gym, but the shrill whistle just inches from my ear breaks the rhythm, the pattern, the words, and the ball rolls off into a corner, hits the wall by a lunch bench locked up for later, when the gym will turn back into the cafeteria. I look around at my classmates, a few of whom stare back at me openly with puzzlement that mirrors my own.

"What's wrong with you?" the gym teacher shouts, crouching so his face is level with mine, and the background closes in and the voices grow louder and I am in gym class; it's winter, we're inside, we're shooting baskets again. The other kids shift nervously; I notice a few seem relieved that I am the object of the anger this time, which tends to hone in on one child at a time, not on the messy group as a whole. I look right at the gym teacher, hold his gaze with mine, praying his face will reveal my mistake so I can at the very least make some sense of what has happened, prevent it from ever happening again. Where had that time gone? What had I done?

I don't know, I answer myself, but another voice, a voice I've been pushing aside more and more, a voice that so often disagrees with how I feel, what I think, what I say, speaks up louder, with greater force and conviction. Yes you do, this strong voice says. You know what you did, it says knowingly, and I put my hands to my ears, but the voice isn't outside my head, can't be shut out. You disappeared, it insists. You gave in.

I remembered this today, when someone asked where I'd been in the middle of a conversation we were having at the time. Losing myself is so second nature to me by now that I'm always surprised when it's noticed by others. "Right here," I wanted to answer, "right here," but I know by now that it won't necessarily mean to them what it means to me, so again, for what seems like the millionth time, I just smile and shrug.

"This is not me," I had said long ago, as I bounced that mottled brown ball in a world of my own, a world in which even the slightest movement I made was possibly wrong, out of the ordinary, conspicuously strange. "This is not me," I had thought reassuringly, wanting to convince all of me that parts of me didn't do things that didn't make sense: How could they, how could that be? But now I know different, know what that voice had been trying to tell me, know that nothing—not words or numbers or people or anything at all, really—makes sense in the same way to all of us, and that knowing that is more important than knowing almost anything else.

"That was me," I say now, feeling the sounds in my mouth, holding my back straight in my chair, my hands still on the table, remembering how it felt to be so small and so scared, so determined and yet so unable to make my mind work the way that I wanted it to, knew that it could. "This is me," says the voice, out of nowhere, and I recognize it immediately, and suddenly it isn't the voice but my voice, and something ineffable clicks into place.

This is me, I say, softly at first, then again, louder, with full knowledge of both the resignation and the triumph the 3/3 phrase represents:

This is me.

PROLOGUE

I am crazy.

But maybe I am not.

Six, twelve, thirty-six times a day, this thought has run through my head for most of my life. When I was finally diagnosed with Tourette's syndrome and concomitant obsessive-compulsive disorder at the age of twenty-four, I wasn't sure which half to hold on to: Did my newly named but congenital neurological conditions merely affirm my insanity or lift the label altogether?

I'm ashamed to confess that I expected this book to practically write itself. The first time I tackled the subject of Tourette's and OCD on paper, not long after my diagnosis, the words spilled out as if they'd been waiting all their lives for the opportunity. Later, after minor revisions, an edited and condensed version of this first stream-of-consciousness essay was published in a women's magazine, accompanied by two unrecognizable photos of me with severely plucked eyebrows, a '60s hair flip, and a glaring headline I shuddered to imagine staring out at my family and friends: "I Watch Myself Do Things I Know Are Crazy."

My husband pointed out that the typeface, in obvious

cahoots with the words, created an effect of fingernails on the wall of a locked ward in an insane asylum. To be fair, the headline was excerpted from the article; the words were mine, and more—they are true. But in spite of what I'd told the editors of this particular magazine, in what I now recognize as a single-minded mission to achieve publication, I was *not* prepared for this singular message to be released at large, for the words "myself" and "crazy" to appear so close to each other in damning, irrevocable boldface. As I walked by the seemingly infinite number of newsstands on the streets of Manhattan I turned away, waiting for the day the issues would be replaced by next month's obliterating batch.

When I talk about Tourette's and OCD, even now, my tics and rituals intensify until I can no longer suppress them. It's as if my brain has a mind of its own, can't flip inside-out and focus so squarely on itself. As it turns out, when I *write* about Tourette's, with any measure of introspection and perspective, the tics and rituals reach heights I'd never imagined. Ordinary objects assume powers their makers never intended; a computer keyboard becomes an unsolvable maze, a hard drive the source of an infinite number of organizational systems, each as incomplete and unsatisfying as the next. While I type the alphabet, line after line of it, or balance each letter with its correspondent on the opposite side of the keyboard, all of which must be duly erased, I flex my feet in a synchronized circle of sorts: first to the left, then down, to the right, up and over again. When I realize the circles have been uniformly counterclockwise, I estimate the total number of circles completed and reverse direction until I've compensated for the imbalance: Symmetry is omnipotent. If I am listening to music, as I often do when I write, my feet flex to the beat—speed up for fast songs, slow down for slow ones. Whenever I am told that I seem adept at doing several things at once, as happens frequently, I always think: You have *no* idea. Writing, the deliberate act of sitting in a defined locale with a particular purpose, pens in the tics, but confinement makes them bold; the angled wrist, usually easy to conceal, becomes a full-fledged fling; my eyes roll back so far the irises virtually disappear.

Some days I awoke at seven to write and found myself twelve hours later planted in front of a blank computer screen; when I tried to remember how I'd occupied all the hours in between I came up perpetually empty. Half the time I sat typing—when the words *did* come—I wasn't even facing the keyboard, my body so twisted and turned with the strain. A tic that often requires me to verbalize—uncensored—every thought that passes through my brain had a cluttering effect on the page; later I went through the manuscript and edited out extraneous, utterly irrelevant details included solely due to my compulsion to commemorate them, such as the type of jam I'd spread on a muffin or the brand name of my current shampoo. Obsessions and compulsions that had faded into so much background thanks to a combination of drugs and behavioral therapy crept back and gathered around me in a most unwelcome dysfunctional family reunion; sometimes, when Ben returned from work, I'd be crouched in a corner scrubbing an inch-square patch of the parquet floor with a toothbrush, convinced that its spotless gleam—if nothing else—would ensure a productive tomorrow. Other days, when I tried to work, I'd become suddenly consumed with personal grooming; if I left the apartment to pick up the paper or a Coke I'd be self-manicured, pedicured, and fully made-up—not to mention free from so much as a single innocent ball of lint, having occupied a good hour plucking minuscule dust buds from my sweater and pants.

When I wasn't writing, I was thinking about writing, and my brain knew it. Over the months of work, I carefully alphabetized my books, CDs, and copious supply of take-out menus and condensed all the little bottles of moisturizer in the apartment into a single, large container. Periodically I discarded all the ice cubes that didn't have a partner in the ice cube tray, forcing myself not to mind too much if an odd number was left melting in the sink. One day I took eleven baths, forcing myself to dunk in an obligatory twelfth before collapsing in bed, all too willing to sacrifice my skin for the sake of "making it even."

The Tourette Syndrome Association, an organization I wholeheartedly recommend for all those in search of the most up-to-date information and invaluable support, defines Tourette's as a "chronic, usually lifelong, neurobiologically based medical condition characterized by involuntary movements (motor tics) and involuntary sounds (vocal tics)." Several neurochemical systems have been implicated in the disorder, including dopamine, serotonin, and norepinephrine. The National Institute of Mental Health estimates that 200,000 Americans have full-blown Tourette's, but the TSA thinks the number could be significantly higher; three-quarters of sufferers are male.

The NIMH also estimates that at least 50 percent of those with Tourette's have obsessive-compulsive disorder, like me. Obsessive-compulsive disorder, commonly called OCD, is a lifelong condition identified by two groups of symptoms: obsessions and compulsions. It is thought to affect as many as one person in forty in the general population, meaning most people know an afflicted person, whether he or she is aware of the illness or not. Like Tourette's, OCD occurs in people of both genders, in every known culture and race, and all over the world. Its most frequent indicators are an irrepressible need for symmetry and order, hoarding and saving, repetitive rituals, nonsensical doubts, superstitious fears, and intrusive thoughts of a religious or sexual nature, but that list should be considered little more than a launching pad; OCD has more gradations than mica.

Until I was twenty-four, Tourette's and obsessive-compulsive disorder meant nothing to me. They were clinical terms, as unrelated to my life as the advertisements on the subway for third-rate plastic surgeons or the symbols on the stock market pages in the business section of the newspaper. Now I am more watchful: inclusive. I pay attention to the details, even those I can't apply to my own present. You never know when a new layer's going to build up or flake off, leaving you with an unrecognizable surface for all the world to see and evaluate.

Everyone has a story, a frame assigned as a birthright in which to arrange the events of a life, the particular thoughts and experiences that are theirs and theirs alone. Not everyone gets to choose it wholly herself.

one —————————————————

SHADES *of* GROUCHO

As I stood outside the imposing front doors of New York City's Hospital for Joint Diseases, I bounced up and down on the balls of my feet in a halfhearted attempt to keep warm. My eyes were watering from the wind, and I could feel ice crystals forming on my eyelashes and the ends of my still shower-damp hair. For ten minutes I'd been trying intermittently—and desperately—to convince Bryant that we should not, after all, go in.

"Is it for diseases of the joints," I asked, trying my hardest to make the question sound provocative, "or for people who've got two diseases, like leukemia and, say, diabetes?" Bryant rolled his eyes.

"Five past," he said.

Now we were late.

A man swallowed by his enormous overcoat walked by

us and into the lobby, and I scanned his profile as he passed. Was he with the Tourette Syndrome Association, I wondered? Was he in fact a regular at the monthly meeting that had seemed like a much better idea back in the relative warmth and familiarity of my apartment uptown? Was I minutes away from learning his preference—even numbers or odd?—and bearing witness as he blinked or sniffed or jerked his limbs akimbo in ways that I would maybe know all too well? Impossible to tell. He looked normal, what I could make of him under that coat, but then again, so did we.

I could see my breath—it was that cold—and Bryant, for some incomprehensible reason, was lacking in hat and in scarf. He wouldn't last much longer. It was time for the big pitch. "What do you say we just go out to dinner? My treat."

For the first time all evening, Bryant looked mildly intrigued. I imagined us splurging on a bottle of red wine at the Union Square Cafe's welcoming bar and laughing conspiratorially about our lucky escape. A nice cabernet or the loony bin: It seemed as simple as that to me then, in spite of the hours I'd spent imagining all the fascinating people I'd meet in the group who also just happened to have Tourette's, people who with wit, eloquence, and engrossing personal histories would dispel my deepest fears and serve as living proof of the theory I'd been touting in public for a while, since I'd perused a book on the subject at Barnes and Noble, that many great artists—Van Gogh, for one, and Sylvia Plath—had suffered from what the world called "madness" but what was really just a blessed surplus of creativity.

My reverie came to an unceremonious halt when

Bryant swilled the dregs of his soda, deposited the can in the garbage can on the sidewalk, and turned and walked inside without a backward glance, leaving me alone in front of the hospital. I watched through the glass, shivering, as he exchanged words with the receptionist at the long front desk and headed over to an elevator bank. When he pressed the button to go up, I buckled. "I'm with him," I told the woman he'd spoken with as I rushed by her, wincing each time my heavy bag smacked into my semifrozen hip. I wasn't suddenly, miraculously, ready to face the unknown quantity of the meeting, but the thought of standing there alone slowly freezing from the outside-in was by far the worse of two evils; it seemed urgent suddenly, a matter of life and death somehow, not to let Bryant out of my sight.

"Floor thirteen," I heard the receptionist call out, as the elevator doors slid shut, but Bryant had already pushed it. In the elevator, the number glowed ominously on the panel, and it occurred to me that I've always heard most buildings don't have a floor thirteen because people are "too superstitious." The irony was almost funny. I knew what floor we were supposed to go to anyway; I'd practically memorized the instructions the group's facilitator had left on my answering machine in a too-warm tone that fell just short of its desired effect: to make me think I was being invited to an exclusive party, a ceremonious event of some prestige. Great—now *she* knows, I couldn't help but think of the receptionist. A hospital is just the kind of place in which I like to "pass." In my experience, most people feel relief, not compassion, most intensely in a hospital; it's certainly true for me, and even when I am seeking treatment of some kind myself and not just visiting, I always experience inevitable self-congratulatory pangs at my own generally good health. I thought about asking Bryant his opinion on the appropriation of "passing" as related to Tourette's, but when I looked over it was clear that panic had rendered him incapable of semantic debate. His eyes were blinking worse than I'd ever seen, forcefully and rapid-fire, and his sniffing was worse than the blinks. On most days, his signature tics are taken for allergy symptoms; no allergy could have provoked these movements. My sinuses veritably ached for him; sniffing that intensely and rapidly results in piercing pain leading directly to disorienting light-headedness. It was also true that group therapy, as a concept, was even more alien to Bryant than to me; I would have bet my savings account he didn't know a single person in his Alabama hometown who'd ever been to see a shrink one-on-one, let alone with a bunch of other would-be wackos. When the bell dinged, signifying our arrival, I set all thoughts of Bryant's certain culture shock aside, however; on the thirteenth floor, there would be no passing for either one of us.

AT SIX, BRYANT had shown up at my place and made polite conversation with Ben and Nicole, my then fiancé and our roommate, both of whose interest in our intended destination had become a little too prurient for my liking over the course of the preceding week. Alone on the sidewalk I breathed a sigh of relief, free at last from the specimen tray. Bryant, whatever his faults or neuroses, was guaranteed not to ask me idiotic questions about group therapy in general and this group therapy in particular, questions like: How are you going to talk to each other if you're all ticcing at the same time? And, more annoying, Will you try to remember the good tics so you can do them for us later?

Generally, I am good about jokes. Sometimes I even encourage them, as a simultaneous means of diffusing tension and appearing well adjusted. Ben and Nicole, and Caroline and Alison, my oldest friend and sister, respectively, take it for granted that my tics are open territory and accuse me of princess-posturing at the slightest complaint. As much as I hate to admit it, they've each developed and fine-tuned an ability to distinguish between manipulative self-pity and genuine despair. But I'd stopped asking them to help with my behavioral therapy because they clearly derived an excess of pleasure in serving as the human equivalents of rubber bands on my wrist. I gritted my teeth when they provided frequent "helpful" status reports and unsolicited constructive reminders—"It's pretty bad tonight (Thanks so much, I wasn't aware of it), did you take your medication?"—or called me Twitchy or Sniffy as if it were the cleverest thing they'd ever thought up. I mustered up a reasonable facsimile of a smile when they held contests to determine who was best able to imitate particular tics, scrunching up their faces and thrashing their heads and hands around in what I considered a travesty of an impression at best. But somehow they hadn't seemed to realize this was different. Different from talking about Tourette's with them or our other close friends, different from discussing it as subject matter in a writing workshop, different even from writing about it, guardedly, in a national magazine, different from anything I'd ever experienced.

In retrospect, I can see that I somehow equated my attendance at group therapy with a public "coming out," the best expression to describe what I mean—as always, the language created in response to prejudice is by necessity needle-sharp. Actively aligning myself with other Tourette's sufferers seemed irrevocable, a scarlet "T" stamped permanently on my forehead, an assignation I would never again have the option to ignore. Up to this point, my disorders had been private, discrete, a part of me I could choose to reveal or not, and I usually chose not. Of course they weren't really private, by the strict definition of the word, since I'd written that article and had been twitching in one way or another for almost twenty years, but they had been a matter of open discourse thus far only between me, my family, my closest friends, and those with a professional interest, such as doctors and therapists.

Even before I knew what they were I tended to dissociate myself from my tics and obsessive-compulsive behaviors. I discussed them disinterestedly, as if they were characteristics of somebody else: a casual acquaintance, a friend of a friend. This is partly a defense mechanism, partly an intellectual exercise, partly because I like to discuss everything this way: one step removed; I was, after all, born and bred in Massachusetts, where the roots of Puritanism have taken profound and permanent hold. Relatives and friends I saw only occasionally took their cues from me and steered clear of the subject overall—if there's one thing I've learned the hard way, it's that most people tiptoe around matters of the mind. Even meeting Bryant, whose symptoms and experiences have been so similar to mine, did not break my illusion of separateness: Bryant too liked to "pass"—like me, had spent a lifetime trying not to stand out in any ways but good ones. This "group"—as I'd called it when I told my father about it, in an effort to make it sound recreational, clublike, even—would be my first interaction with a parallel world I knew existed but had tried so hard to avoid. These would be people who *knew*.

I'D KEPT THE Tourette Syndrome Association newsletter advertising the group therapy meetings and tucked it into the daily planner my father sends me each year with great hope in his heart, instead of throwing it away or filing it in one of the many files I maintain doggedly but never look through. I figured maybe I could sneak in sometime and make myself invisible in the back of the room, like the kids who'd always appeared an extension of their seats in my college art history seminar; like them, I could absorb enough by osmosis to make the experience worthwhile, avoiding genuine participation entirely. My main problem was this: I seriously questioned my ability to open myself up to a group of people who wouldn't, or rather couldn't, accept my party line: that Tourette's and OCD were really just so fascinating when you knew about them that I was almost *glad* I had them. It seems too new-agey, I told Bryant, when I showed him the newsletter. It wasn't that I was scared, I explained, it was just that I hated groups of any kind. I wasn't a joiner, never had been, and the people who actually showed up at these meetings were surely in much worse shape than us. For all we knew, they were institutionalized, let out for the evening on nutcase parole. Maybe they were dangerous.

The truth was I'd grown comfortable self-assessing my disorders as a rarefied burden that defied real comprehension, except by Bryant of course, who being so like me in so many ways only fed into and fostered both the exclusivity and the delusion. I wasn't quite sure how I'd react when anyone other than Bryant gained access to the thick-walled, windowless compartment in which I stored any messy, potentially alarming thoughts about Tourette's or OCD— the disorder's frequent tag-along companion—my sizable cache of humiliating, devastating, or otherwise too-painful-to-think-about experiences. I wasn't ready to dig up, dust off, and dissect my memories of the times I'd been stared at on the subway, edged away from at a bus stop or in line at the grocery store, pointed at outright by a whispering unthinking child. And I was positive I didn't want to be closely linked with some of the characters I'd conjured up in my mind's eye; I had images of situations where I'd be at a nice restaurant with, say, my new in-laws, and a vituperate, red-faced Tourettic monster I'd met in "group" would approach, spewing profanities and knocking plates off the table with abandon. These little scenes usually ended with all of us being thrown out of the restaurant and one of the non-Tourettic characters backing away from me with raised hands while saying to the others "It's really such a shame. She looks so . . . *normal.*"

Outside the elevator, about twelve people were milling around a door that was apparently locked. I'd been instructed via my answering machine to look for the "Garden Room." A small plaque on the door confirmed that we were in the right place; in my mind I conjured the scene on the other side of the door—garden was really a euphemism for zoo, I decided, one of those new, politically correct zoos where the animals—in this case, us—were allowed to roam outside of cages in a simulation of their original habitat so visitors could maintain the soothing illusion of freedom and natural order.

"I'm going to the bathroom," Bryant and I announced simultaneously, and dove for the doors, conveniently located right by the elevators. I entered the first open stall and locked the door behind me. Sitting on the closed toilet, I checked my pulse: depressingly regular, even on the slow side. I have pulse-taking down to a science—I turn my watch so the face is in on the inside of my wrist—and I can detect the slightest change in its normal pace; the concentration the act demands is a preferred calming technique of mine, as deep breathing makes me feel faint, and faintness makes me nervous, thereby negating the intended effect. Rest room stalls are in themselves calming, for the unadulterated solitude they represent; they're one of the few places in this world where privacy is still virtually guaranteed. This one was on the cleaner side of average, I noted with approval; the white-tiled floor was slightly grungy, but no teenagers had defaced the pale pink sides or door with inane, ungrammatical graffiti, and the hook meant for a coat or purse was shiny and intact. I sat there, twitching unselfconsciously, mostly my neck and hands, until I heard the door to the men's room creak open and shut. Out in the hallway someone spoke to Bryant, who answered back. I heard my name. Clenching my fists to control the more expansive tics, I unlocked the stall, let loose one massive neck twitch that cracked so loudly I worried for a moment that I'd finally snapped something, and stepped out into the hallway.

A gaunt blond woman with a feathered 1970s hairstyle and blank eyes was standing with Bryant by the water fountain, and when I approached she took a giant step toward me, standing too close. "Are you on meds? Are you on meds?" she asked twice in rapid succession. Up close I could see she was middle-aged; I'd thought she was younger. Her eyes weren't blank, I decided, but off-kilter in some other way. One appeared to be frozen in place. I looked at Bryant, but judging by the expression on his face she'd stumped him too. Suddenly I got it—they said meds on TV, it meant medication—although I'd never heard the term used in real life.

"Yes," I answered, stretching out the syllable, deciding how much to reveal. "Prozac and Haldol," I added, surprising myself. I rarely told people about the Haldol, as anybody who's heard of it thinks schizophrenia, an association I can do without. She didn't blink; I might as well have said aspirin. A pair of men about my age who'd been eavesdropping from the other side of the hall joined our awkward trio.

"I've tried Haldol. How many milligrams?" one of them asked in a friendly voice, as if inquiring after a recipe. Were there no boundaries in this world? I didn't care. It felt liberating to lay it all out on the table for a change. I half wished I had something more exotic to offer up, electroshock treatments or bleeding by leech.

"Do you have Tourette's? Do you both have Tourette's?" the blond woman asked before I could provide my current dosage, taking yet another step forward; by this point we were standing so close we looked like refugees from some long-ago game of sardines-in-a-can. Bryant took a step back and managed a pleasant if faltering smile. He gestured toward the woman.

"This is Joan," he half squeaked, his voice noticeably higher than usual. "And Joan, this is Amy. And yes, we both have Tourette's." I rolled my eyes. Typical: Bryant insisted on protocol even when interacting with the insane. Obviously we both had Tourette's, or we wouldn't be there; was Joan under the impression her disorder had groupies? And we were both twitching so badly—our tried-and-true standbys: sniffing and blinking for Bryant, neck and jaw cracks for me—that I wondered if the question itself had been some kind of a tic. That I could understand; one of the questions I was eager to ask once and if the meeting ever began was if other people had much trouble controlling what they said, not in terms of random outbursts, but extreme impulsivity, in otherwise ordinary conversations. I was constantly accused of asking and then insisting on receiving answers to questions that were idiotic, irrelevant, inappropriate, or obvious; I felt guilty when I realized how quickly and harshly I'd judged Joan based on appearance alone: that hair, those eyes. Maybe we were actually kindred spirits, fellow big-mouths with a common lack of the inhibition Tourette's steals away, an equally tenuous and sporadic hold on something as elemental to most people as the spoken word.

An older man, in his early sixties, approached, hand extended. "Have we all met?" he said, shaking our hands. "Joan, Patrick, Michael, would you do me the honor of introducing me to your new friends?" His speech was clipped, British without the accent.

"I'm Amy, and this is Bryant," I supplied when no one else spoke; Patrick and Michael hadn't yet been introduced to us, nor we to them, so we shook hands too. "This is our first time," I added, feeling goofy and virginal but hoping someone other than Joan would decide to take us under a wing and provide some relevant information, such as who was in charge and when we were going to start. The waiting was getting to me; I could feel tension building in the joints and muscles of my shoulders, neck, torso, and arms, the half of my body that bears the brunt of most of my tics. My legs are by far my most reliable part—the least likely component to malfunction and develop an independent agenda from the rest of me. The older man, Tom, whom I'd designated the professor on sight, took out his wallet and distributed business cards. He was, in fact, a professor, at a college in the Bronx; I breathed a sigh of relief at this small yet certain indication of allegiance with the world of the sane. Joan and the two younger men thrust the cards without looking deep into the pockets of their jeans. I wondered if they'd received them before.

"Oh, boy," the man whose name was apparently Pat sputtered in the non-sequitur pattern I was beginning to catch the knack of. "My obsessions have been out of control." He jerked his head suddenly backward, and we all waited, politely, for him to finish. I'd noticed in the mere minutes since we'd arrived that regardless of other, self-evident strangeness, people with Tourette's knew how to talk to other people with Tourette's, knew instinctively to wait for the end of interrupted sentences, faced visible tics head-on without so much as a flinch. My own sometimes aggressive, confrontational manner of speaking can be partly attributed to the fact that for twenty years I've had to tolerate having my sentences finished—usually inaccurately—by others, who assume, wrongly, that I'm searching for words. Tics are uninvited guests who frequently show up mid-thought or conversation: On the telephone, several times a week, I am hung up on by people who aren't used to the involuntary nuances of my speech patterns, and all of my closest friends and family are guilty of this sin, assuming a "yes" or a "no" before I am capable of spitting it out. As someone who thinks and speaks quickly when not midtic, I can certainly relate to the frustration others experience when waiting through my apparently unfounded silences, but it was going to be gratifying, I could tell, not to have to apologize for the unavoidable swallowed words.

Finally Pat was ready. "It's hard for me to work when most days I can't even leave my place with all the crap I've got to do. You guys know what I mean." And I did. That very evening I'd been waiting for Bryant by the door with my bag over my shoulder and my heavy coat on, feet planted firmly on the floor to avoid distraction by any tics or rituals that would thwart our departure, such as arranging loose coins by type, in stacks of a dollar each, or emptying the refrigerator and placing the contents back in by food group, in a way that ensured all the staples were totally inaccessible but that met some standard of order I craved. For important appointments I generally gave myself an hour's headstart at the least, in an attempt to arrive exactly on time; I'd developed a repertoire of convincing excuses over the years for those occasions when I, too, couldn't get out the front door.

"I'm going to start volunteering at an old-timers' program," Pat continued. "They won't mind there if I jerk around." My hands, in tightly clenched fists again, were distracting me. They were also starting to ache. I flexed them at the wrists, extending and bending my fingers a few times, but as always the energy found another outlet. My neck started twitching, as if I had a burning itch on my cheek that could only be scratched by my shoulder. When I could, I looked around, but no one was staring or, more surprising, pretending not to. No one said a word to me, in fact, not "Gee, that must really hurt," or "You'll dislocate your shoulder doing that." They were lost in their own thoughts, drinking from the water fountain, counting change for the soda machine I'd noticed by the rest rooms, waiting for Pat to start talking again. *That makes you look crazy,* I heard faintly in my head, but it was a voice from a long time ago that seemed newly out of place, and I brushed it aside. With no one to snap at or explain to, my own tics faded into so much background.

"Are you going to be volunteering at a nursing home?" I asked Pat, who was scrunching up his face and unscrunching it, a tic of the unsightly genre I fight at all costs in public, as its distortion is impossible to mask or explain away, and making jerky little kicks to the side with his right foot. "I didn't know they had them in New York. In the city." No response. Joan was banging her left elbow repetitively against the water cooler. After one resounding bang she looked right at me, as much as she could with her frozen eye and the left side of my head nearly parallel to the ground. Pat's face-scrunching had struck a nerve—in front of very few people do I ever let myself look like that.

"He must mean a nursing home, a nursing home. He doesn't always get things right," Joan stage-whispered, although Pat was standing right there where he'd been all along, well within earshot. "Right, Pat? You mean a nursing home, a nursing home. Right, Pat?" Her long thin pale hands twisted around each other as she spoke, the fingers occasionally separating from the swirling mass. I couldn't take my eyes off them; my hand tics never looked like that— fluid, like seaweed underwater. It occurred to me that maybe this wasn't a tic. I'd assumed the tics would be obvious, easy to distinguish from deliberate statements or movements, but I'd assumed wrong. It was the Mad Hatter's tea party, and I was both Alice and the Hatter—all rules applied, and no rules applied; I was crazy but also painfully sane. In the general spirit of intrusiveness, I readied myself to ask Joan: Was she aware of her hands?

"No." Pat shouted, when he emerged from an extended bout with the face and the foot. "Old-timers!"

"I think he's saying Alzheimer's," Bryant said to me and Joan, but before Pat could confirm or deny, the elevator doors dinged again, and a woman my parents' age in a turquoise, oversized shirt and black leggings strode confidently out, clapping her hands and gushing apologies. I recognized her voice; she was the group's facilitator, Norma, who'd sounded so overly ecstatic on my machine at the prospect of Bryant's and my attendance that I'd almost reconsidered. Unbridled enthusiasm in others makes me uncomfortable; in conjunction with Tourette's and its toxic levels of unharnessed energy, it had frightened me.

Norma unlocked the door, and we were swept into a white-walled, gray-carpeted conference space. Bryant and I took seats next to each other in the semicircle of plastic chairs directly opposite Norma, who looked more like a 1960s stewardess than the strict, spare, buttoned-up Freudian I'd half hoped for. Who'd *choose* to hang out with a bunch of loony twitchers? Nicole had joked, and Norma was apparently the unexpected punch line. As if on cue, she plunked down a heaving grocery bag on the floor in front of her. "I've got bagels," she exclaimed cheerily, and a few people came forward and accepted raw, unadorned bagels on festively colored paper napkins. The guy on my right leaned over, put his hand square on my thigh, and whispered, "What kind of person brings bagels and no cream cheese? My grandmother would turn in her grave." I nodded—I'd been thinking the same thing, not to mention that it was dinnertime, and pizza would have been a far more welcome contribution—and then registered belatedly the wayward hand. I froze, but before I could say or do anything about it he'd removed it; the whole episode lasted only an instant. Had it actually happened, or had I finally lost all contact with my Alice half?

While I was trying to remember if I'd read anything about hallucinations as a side effect of either of my current medications, the guy on the other side of Bryant leaned across him and gently smacked my leg, just where the first guy had. After a second that seemed longer, he too jerked his hand away. "I think we're freaking her out, Tony," he said to the guy who'd first touched me, laughing as he punched the floor, palmed the top of Bryant's head, and sat back in his chair; when I mustered up the nerve to check him out seconds later he looked bored, impatient for the meeting to start. Tony, who'd seemed mildly offended by my startled reaction to his touch, was drumming his fingers on his thigh, humming to himself as if nothing out of the ordinary had transpired.

Bryant, who'd been watching with fascination, finally jumped in. "That's a tic, right?" he asked the man sitting next to him. "The touching?" I don't know why it hadn't oc-curred to me too. Bryant is more of a toucher than I am, but Southern upbringings seem to encompass physical affection as early and effortlessly as infants assume a preference for either the right hand or the left. Although I was quite familiar with touching tics, my own and Bryant's, when my own involves touching other people it is usually surreptitious. For example, it is a rare subway ride when I'm not compelled to brush my hand against a suede coat or a furry, dangling scarf, even a wayward lock of hair, but these tics can be released without attracting attention, even by wearer of said coat or scarf, the person attached to the hair. I say compelled because the touching is never about desire, has nothing to do with wanting to touch and everything to do with needing to; as often as not, the object of my touching compulsion is repugnant or filthy or both: a wad of ancient gum stuck to the edge of a homeless person's tattered sweater, a patch of mud on the side of a stranger's sweat-soaked sneaker. If I get caught, as happens every so often, a murmured "Excuse me" always precipitates an understanding smile. The New York subway system is usually so crowded that any unwanted contact is interpreted as par for the course, and I don't look like either a pervert or a physical threat. Bryant touches everyone a lot, on the subway and otherwise—he is one of the few huggers I can stomach—but as I've said, it's a Southern trait; he's doubly predisposed.

"Yes, it's a tic," the man answered in crescendo. "And so's this, and this, and this!" He leapt off his chair to chuck the shoulders and grab the foot of a man across from him in the circle, a man whose subsequent expression of horror led me to believe he too was new to the group and afflicted chiefly with self-contained, noninteractive tics. "I should come with a warning," he added. "Faulty Wiring! Likely to Explode! Although of course it's nobody's business. Right?" Bryant and I quickly agreed—although I prayed my ready assent wouldn't target me as a receptive candidate for regular pokes, pats, and prods. Sometimes an uninvited, even inadvertent touch is enough to make me twitch for hours, especially if it causes my clothing to rub against my skin, shifting my carefully constructed protective shell. Imagine you have no skin, are an amorphous mass of tissue and blood vessels and pulsing organs; to be touched would be intolerable, an invitation for disease or the irrevocable transformation for the worse of a patch of your physical essence. Or better yet, picture your skin as comprised only of nerve endings with no neutral ground; in this case, the barely discernible pat of a fingertip would send sensations vibrating through every atom in your body. Welcome to Tourette's.

Looking around the circle, my right foot tapping rapid-fire to hold off any major, more obvious tics, I took a head count. Although I knew from my reading that Tourette's was far more common in males than in females, the ratio was jarring in person. With the exceptions of Joan and Norma, I was the only woman in the room. The men ranged in age from early twenties to late sixties, and only a few could have been mental ward patients based solely on appearance (a misbuttoned shirt, stained and wrinkled pants, something off about the eyes), I was relieved to note. On the opposite end of the spectrum from these were the oldest two men, Tom, the professor, who'd earlier distributed business cards, and the other, a graphic designer who was assessing the rest of us disdainfully, as if he'd read my mind and disagreed with my mental ward count; evidently his would have been higher. As Norma packed up the remaining bagels, the man who'd been chucked on the shoulder asked in a loud voice if the doctors were going to be allowed to remain. After a few moments of confusion, it was established that the tweedy older men were not medical professionals of any kind but Tourette's sufferers like the rest of us, there to participate. The professor took the opportunity to pass out more of his cards. The graphic designer managed a thin smile. A couple of people watched them suspiciously until the professor let out a loud hoot followed by a guttural screech. Coprolalia: the involuntary outburst of obscenities or other socially inappropriate words or phrases; 10 to 15 percent of sufferers are affected. It was the first time I'd seen it up close. Needless to say, he was in.

"Why don't we go around the circle and introduce ourselves," Norma suggested, in a transparent attempt to establish order. It was hard to pay attention to anything or anyone; the room shimmered with movement. A few head and neck twitches, very much like mine. Lots of blinking and sniffing, like Bryant's, some hand and foot jerking, a fair amount of aimless murmuring, an occasional blast of clear, pure sound. Through the buzz and commotion and disinterest, Norma persevered. "I see some new faces out there I'd like to get to know." She winked at me. Not a tic, I registered; Norma must feel at these meetings like I do most of the time out in the world, I realized—her effortless stillness made her conspicuous here: an outsider. Pat's lower leg flew up and out in response to some nonexistent reflex test. Tic. The man seated on the other side of Bryant went first. He was a photojournalist named Lowell Handler. I hadn't recognized him, but when he spoke I realized I'd seen him before, at a Museum of Natural History–sponsored screening of *Twitch and Shout,* a documentary film on Tourette's he associate-produced. I was surprised and secretly comforted to find Lowell mingling with the likes of us, although as far as I knew there wasn't a group of more socially prominent Touretters for him to join. I had suspected, when watching his film, that he too fancied himself primarily a member of the rest of the world.

Joan was an office manager, "single but looking," a self-professed veteran of the group. Pat, too, had been coming for years; he was my age, twenty-eight, and had never been able to hold down a job, due more to the crippling obsessive-compulsive disorder that kept him largely housebound than to his physical tics, which were minor in comparison. Bryant had been right; he was about to start volunteering with Alzheimer's patients—he pronounced it distinctly this time—and I tried not to look at Bryant. I knew I would laugh if I did; I had no doubt he too was thinking that thrusting Tourettic volunteers on Alzheimer's sufferers was someone's really bad idea. If you were literally losing your mind, the last thing you needed was to be constantly exposed to people who by virtue of bizarre movements and sounds would make you think you were degenerating even faster than you actually were. Stan worked at a drugstore. He was thirty, stocky and blond, with an affected voice that suggested a certain upbringing. Sure enough, he was from Greenwich; his parents hated him, he added casually, as an afterthought, interrupting Mike, who'd already started his own introductory spiel. Mike was young, "past twenty," he said, but I suspected not much. He was a student/filmmaker, from New York, original home of the trust-funded ambiguous "vocation." His father, he declared as his right eye rolled back in his head over and over, was a Very Wealthy Man. Mike was also single, he made a point of telling us; again, I fought eye contact with Bryant—we were now at the Mad Hatter's dating service, it seemed. I half expected the professor, whose turn it was next, to supply his pant size and daily workout routine.

Timmy was the last to introduce himself; I knew he was Timmy because Pat had tried to speak for him earlier. "That's Timmy," he'd said at the end of his own introduction, gesturing formally, palm up, the affection in his voice nearly palpable. "He won't want to talk, so I'm telling you now." But Norma had tut-tutted this.

"Timmy's turn will come," she'd said. "Now where were we?" When it was finally Timmy's turn, he seemed not only unlikely to talk but physically incapable of speech. Words were getting stuck in his throat and staying there; I empathized, although I'd never experienced such an obvious, full-fledged pile-up. You could almost see the syllables rising and smashing against each other like angry whitecaps; combined, they were creating a gurgle deep in his throat.

"It's okay, Timmy," Pat encouraged, glaring at Norma. "You're doing great." My foot-tapping sped up, and my hands started to jerk, unobtrusively at first, then harder and faster. Timmy was an underdog by nature, he exuded it; you wanted to root for him, but it went deeper than that for me and, I was sure, the rest of the room. Watching him struggle was like stumbling upon a funhouse-mirror version of myself, like covering my eyes with my hands at the gruesome parts of a movie but peeking through the cracks in my fingers. Don't get me wrong—there was nothing voyeuristic about it. We were his teammates, cheering him on for his own sake, but also for the greater good of the team. Before he'd spoken a word it was clear: Timmy belonged. But did *I*?

I felt amorphous, sliding definitively down some self-made evolutionary ladder, from normal, to normal with manageable Tourette's, to one small step from the edge of an abyss. By now Timmy was twitching his body as well as his voice. The tic he was stuck on reminded me of a breakdancing move I remember—"the wave"—in which the arms are extended Jesus-on-the-cross style and an undulating motion passes from the fingers of the left hand up the arm, across the shoulders, and so on down to the fingers of the right hand. Timmy's elbows were bent, making his arms into underdeveloped wings and creating a cerebral palsy effect, but otherwise he had the move down.

We waited, not quite the way we'd waited for Pat. This seemed more urgent; I was actually willing Timmy to speak. I suspected I was not the only first-timer present who was seeing in him the severity of symptoms I'd been spared and grappling with a conflicting response. The room had settled, except for Timmy—the collective focus on him had muted the rest of us; intense concentration or focus often quiets Tourettic tics. Finally he spoke, spitting out the words with equal measures of rage and relief. "Mike's a nigger cock," he said twice, and his jerking slowed until he too was nearly still. I was transfixed, frozen in place on my hard plastic chair. Timmy was cringing, shrinking into himself. Pat sighed a tremendous sigh of relief. I couldn't help myself; I looked at Mike. Emerging from my fog, I realized that most of the circle was giggling. Even Norma was smiling. Mike was laughing harder than anyone.

"That's a new one, Timmy." He sputtered. "But I think you've got the wrong guy!" He held out his big white hands, palms down. "I may be a cock, I've been called worse, but that's all I'll give you this time." Bryant pinched my side, hard. Everything I'd read about this manifestation of copro-lalia—the rarest and most socially unacceptable characteris-tic of Tourette's, yet that with which most people associate the disorder—had done nothing to prepare me for the shock of witnessing it firsthand. This was a whole different ballgame from the professor's hoots and shouts and Lowell's taps and touches. This was the big league, and for years I'd been skulking around in the minors.

Questioning the origins of the outburst was dangerous, I knew. If Tourette's sufferers with coprolalia really meant what they said in their Tourettic outbursts, they would be racist, sexist, vulgar, profoundly disturbed sociopaths rather than victims of errant signals deep within the coils of their brains. But as much as I knew I had no control over my own tics, remembered my most desperate failed attempts to sub-due them, including trying to break my collarbone one summer in the hopes of obtaining and legitimizing an im-mobilizing neck brace and periodically tying my feet to the legs of a chair, I'd always found it hard to believe that actual racial slurs and graphic sexual terms could come from the same dark recesses of the brain that caused my jerks and twitches. Timmy erased my lingering doubts with the first thing I heard him say. The words had come out of nowhere, in response to nothing. His immediate reaction to his out-burst was unfeignable shame. Now he was smiling sheep-ishly, the horrible anticipation over and done with, while Pat rubbed his shoulders soothingly. We moved on.

As it turned out, the introductions took up a good chunk of the hour-and-a-half-long session. This was gener-ally the case. Although nine of the group's participants were "regulars," no one had balked at hearing basic biographical data they must have already known. In fact, more than a couple of times, one of the less severely afflicted regulars actually prompted a speaker to retell a particular story or provide a certain bit of information remembered from a previous gathering. Sometimes this seemed to be done for the benefit of me, Bryant, and the other newcomers and was hallmarked as such. "Pat, not everyone here knows that you've moved back in with your parents. Why don't you talk about that?" the professor would say, looking at me for confirmation of interest. Norma was in an impossible position, and I pitied her—several times she tried to cut short a rambling monologue or anecdote only to be chastened by a regular who'd insist that the speaker go on, in what was obviously a familiar unpleasant dance that left Norma, time and again, with trampled feet. Bryant and I didn't say much on our turns; the other first-timers were equally reticent, and no one pressed us to speak. Somehow it was understood that we needed this first time to soak in the atmosphere, sleep off our jet lag, master the rudiments of the language, just enough to get by. As in any culture, there were rules, some spoken but many more left unsaid.

As a fairly recent graduate of a creative writing program rife with often agonizing workshop-style classes, the patience of these people initially baffled and amazed me. My own eagerness to hear Pat and Mike and Stan—all of whom spoke for long minutes at a shot, losing their train of thought and repeating themselves over and over—came as even more of a surprise. To most people, Stan's memory of the first time his mother slapped him across the face for ticcing, or rather for not stopping ticcing when she asked him to, would be upsetting, a tale with little narrative value illustrative of not much more than bad parenting. To me, listening to Stan create the same scene with few variations in the space of a quarter of an hour was transformative. I'd stumbled upon a branch of my family tree I'd known existed but never expected to meet, and there was so much catching up to do—filling in the blank spots of our common history. After several more sessions I would realize that Stan's first slap, Mike's terrifying stay in a psychiatric ward, the speech the professor gives to his classes each fall explaining his Tourette's—these stories and so many more are our folklore and bear repeating as often as we feel like it; they'd been kept locked up for so long with no outlet it would be a wonder if we ever tired of hearing them. I'd reached into a vacuum so many times myself, in bookstores and libraries and on the Internet, searching and coming up empty, and I'd been luckier than most: I'd found Bryant. What must not knowing have been like for Pat? For Timmy? My reaction was instinctive: After a while, I didn't care what these people were saying, and how many times they said it. I needed to hear.

Lowell was telling us about a woman who'd shouted at him on the street when Timmy murmured something to himself. "What's that, Timmy?" Norma said quickly, obviously annoyed that a few people were dominating the discussion. Timmy's elbows shot up again, winglike.

"Joan looks like Marilyn Manson," he said, with the echo I'd noticed in Joan: "Marilyn Manson." Immediately I visualized the androgynous rocker I'd seen on a magazine cover at a newsstand just that week. As if guided by magnet, every eye in the room turned to Joan. I hadn't laughed at Timmy's previous outburst. I'd felt like it—I'm prone to nervous laughter, and everyone else had been laughing—but it hadn't seemed fair, and the slur itself certainly wasn't funny. But there was no gray territory here. I hadn't noticed it myself, but now I couldn't see how I'd missed it—Joan could be Marilyn Manson's unadorned twin. Of course if the resemblance had occurred to me I wouldn't have said it out loud; it was a stretch, at best, to consider the comparison a compliment. In the heavy pause that followed, Joan looked thoughtful. Then she chuckled, shaking her head in mock dismay, removing a finger from a dam. We all cracked up then, laughed so hard I forgot to catalog tics or notice if anyone was staring at mine. The tension I'd felt in the corners of the room dissipated, and when Joan said, "That's not the way to make friends, Timmy. You should have said Marilyn Monroe, Marilyn Monroe," and the laughter started all over again, it fully dissolved.

I'd imagined—and gathered from what I'd read—that the inappropriate phrases blurted out by those afflicted with coprolalia would be mostly random, like a word or object that appears in a dream, and you know you've heard or seen it somewhere before but it could have been anywhere, on TV or while waiting for the subway, and in your dream it's not at all in its original context. Some of Timmy's vocal tics were like that; perhaps his brain plucked words out of nowhere, but it seemed more likely a case of faulty wiring, words that existed in the dark alleyways of his vocabulary bursting forth on their own. When Timmy later shouted out "Fuck the Wu Tang Clan," I assumed (correctly, it turned out) that he was a music buff—because nothing any of us had said had overtly triggered the reference.

And then there were the vocal tics that didn't seem quite

so arbitrary. Timmy's observation about Joan wasn't in the least bit relevant but it was certainly accurate. And although it could have been a coincidence, it broke the tension that had been building up to that point and allowed us to wind down the meeting as friends. For the rest of the evening, in fact, because the first one had gone over so well, Timmy continued to interrupt the flow of conversation with other comparisons between group members and famous people. They were so on target—and increasingly unflattering—that I began to dread my assignation of a celebrity match. When he did—Diane Keaton—I breathed a sigh of relief. "Not bad," Bryant whispered to me. Not really true, I thought, but there was no doubt Timmy had said it on purpose, regardless of whether or not I was likely to be flattered. The tic had become at least semideliberate, maybe even a comic device.

Coprolalia is like any other tic, controllable to a very limited extent—suppressible is a more accurate word—but ultimately unstoppable. Random and arbitrary, yes—why do I, for example, jerk my neck to one side one minute and then roll my shoulder the next?—but also confined to a finite repertoire. What do we all do, after all, but work within the parameters of our materials and experience? With few exceptions, we have standardized bodies and brains; when things go wrong with them, it makes sense to me that they'd go wrong in comprehensibly wrong ways—wrong movements are tics, motions with no point, black sheep cousins of the hand that reaches over the shoulder to scratch the back, the foot that angles forward, fast and hard, to kick a soccer ball. The wrong words are tics too, real words, familiar words perhaps, but nonsensically assembled and ugly. When a fuse blows in your house, in other words, the paint doesn't start peeling, the lights go off.

The only words Timmy spoke during that meeting that were wholly his own came at the very end of the couple of hours. Lowell and the professor were debating the relative merits of confrontational exchanges with strangers who stared at their tics when Timmy interrupted, looking and sounding much younger than his age, which I guessed to hover near thirty. "My parents hit me," he said, in a quite different voice from the one he'd been shouting in, and Lowell and the professor stopped short. "They hit me a lot when I was a kid." I was stunned to find that Timmy could tell stories, relay sequential thoughts; he'd certainly given no indication of it up to that point. The astonishment delayed the effect of his words, but not for long. His voice grew louder, more forceful, insistent. "They hit me and they locked me in the closet. They said they'd let me out when I stopped acting crazy. After a while I stopped telling them I couldn't stop, and I just stayed in the closet. They used to hit me." A few eyes were misty when he'd finished, and the professor looked furious, wishing, I imagined, he could show Timmy's parents the inside of that closet, but nobody spoke. Someone finally asked Timmy, tentatively, if he thought he could ever forgive them, but he was birdlike again, jerking and mumbling incoherently. I remembered a piece of information provided earlier by Pat: Timmy still lived at home.

Norma, in her first and only decisive move of the night, announced it was time for us all to go home. Bryant and I and the other first-timers were swarmed, given more business cards and slips of paper with numbers and addresses scrawled on them; we were asked for ours, and we signed napkins as if we'd just won Academy Awards. As we filed out of the Garden Room, the professor pulled us away from the huddle forming in the hallway and asked if we'd like to join him and a few of the others for a drink. We demurred, having planned private assessment at a nearby bar, but he insisted, and we soon found ourselves in a diner with the professor and four other Touretters with symptoms of roughly the same moderate severity, at a long table in the main room.

The waitress had asked where we wanted to sit, and I'd automatically pointed to the back—there were hooters and screechers among us, after all—but the professor had authoritatively insisted on the center table, and I'd felt somehow admonished. We ordered, amid a low-pitched chorus of vocalizations and a frenzy of tics (all of us, I noticed, were twitchier now than we'd been at the end of the meeting); the waitress didn't blink an eye, and amazed by what I took to be jadedness, I whispered to Bryant, "Only in New York." Having anticipated the actual purpose of this meal, in spite of the camaraderie I knew we'd all shared earlier in the evening—to reassure ourselves that we were somehow superior to those who had not been invited along—I wasn't surprised when the professor cleared his throat (not a tic) and announced, "I know this is going to sound terribly elitist, but I feel so much better in this group than in that one."

I couldn't argue that I had little in common outside of Tourette's with say, Timmy and Pat, who could be categorized as nonfunctioning in so many ways. They both, for one, receive federal disability funds, as they'd revealed unabashedly during the session, and rightly so. But although in our new smaller group we were all well dressed and clean cut, I could see other tables eyeing us not so surreptitiously;

the professor, in particular, has a distinctive hoot, and the self-consciousness of feeling watched—together we attracted more attention than any of us would have alone—had worsened my tics and probably everybody else's as well. The older couple to my left exchanged raised eyebrows, I noticed, but it was the group of women my own age, seated at the next table, that caused bile to rise in my gut when I saw one make the universal sign of craziness—the index finger circling at the temple—blatantly, as if we were a touring group from a school for the blind. Even in a small, intimate group comprised of individuals sharing a rare neurological disorder, it seemed we were doomed to play out a ruthless process of stratification. We were the "good" Touretters, the ones who didn't appear autistic or retarded, the ones who looked to the outside world just like everybody else. We could sleep soundly at night knowing that even in our darkest moments with Tourette's we had jobs and relationships and the ability to drive a car and converse with strangers, among all the other thousands of things we do each day without thinking twice. We had our disorder "under control." But everything is relative, I wanted to say. People are staring at us, don't you see them? Face it: We're *not* like everybody else. I was glad when it was late enough that we had to leave: "After all, work tomorrow," the professor said pointedly, as he shook hands all around again and strode off down the street with a final hoot.

Although I agreed at the time that it was a relief to have a "normal" conversation after all that madness, as we cabbed uptown in silence, I couldn't forget the way I'd felt watching Lowell—certainly one of the most professionally accomplished members of the group—bounce around the room like an ion, hearing Stan's slapping story, laughing with Joan over the pitfalls of exposing potential suitors to her tics, remembering how much energy I'd exerted over the years to keep men I liked from noticing mine. And later that night, long after I'd told Ben and Nicole I'd tell them about it all some other time and was lying in bed jerking my right foot under the covers so furiously that Ben threatened to sleep on the couch if I didn't stop soon, I found myself thinking about Timmy, not as a freak, not as an object of pity, but as one of the few people I'd ever met who knew all too well what it was like to fight your own body for control every single waking minute of every single day. And I knew then what chilled me most about Timmy's story. I've never been beaten or locked up in my life, but I understood bone-deep the sickening comfort of that prison of a closet.

two ══

BODIES *in* MOTION
STAY *in* MOTION

The summer I was eight, I developed a tic. The studio where I studied ballet four days a week was lined with mirrors on three sides; the fourth side was a wall of windows looking out onto a parking lot. We warmed up facing the mirrors, watching our muscles flex and the lines of our spines, comparing abilities to form and then hold a particular pose. One day, while two of my classmates practiced a center routine and I stood with the other three girls waiting for our turn, my own reflection distracted me from the steps. Every so often, my head tilted to the left in a sort of jerking motion. It felt familiar, as if my head and neck had practiced the move without telling the rest of me, but I'd never actually seen myself doing it before. I held my hands to the sides of my face and pressed in, trying to force my head to stay straight. That seemed to work, but later in the class — after I'd had my turn in the center and we were all gathered in the back of the room to learn a new routine — I felt myself doing it again.

This first tic was a sort of contraction of the muscles in my neck that caused my head to jerk to either the left or the right, rapidly, sometimes twice in succession, several times an hour. The motion was not unlike the first stroke of the shake I use after swimming leaves my ears clogged, and for months I wondered if I had somehow managed to trap water in my head permanently, maybe in the bathtub, although I showed no signs of the sloshing and thickness that made other people's voices sound funny and my own unusually resonant after a trip to the beach or an afternoon in my grandparents' pool. And although it lingered, cropped up periodically like a late-winter cough, for a little while no one else seemed to notice it.

At first I found my new tic a fascinating quirk, not unlike double-jointedness or my sister's coveted ability to roll her eyes all the way back in her head until just the whites were showing. To myself, I called it my twitch. It became something of a game to see how long I could go without making the motion, a game not unlike solitaire, which I played constantly, in that even though sometimes my odds looked good for a while, I never actually won. One day after ballet, however, in the tiny changing room next to the studio, one of my classmates, Leonelle, suddenly yelled, "Stop!" as I was sitting on the bench putting on my regular shoes to go home. I looked up, jarred into reversing my twitch midway. I felt guilty, as if I'd been caught cheating, or in a flagrant lie.

"What's that thing you're doing? With your head?"

I had known the girls in my ballet class for years. We

were the "special development class," hand-selected as the most promising young dancers at the ballet school, the only ones with a legitimate shot—however remote—at becoming professionals. Leonelle was a year older than I; she was the oldest in our group and my chief challenger as leader, with a slight edge, given that she towered over me by nearly a foot and was an only child besides, which meant that she wore special, hand-knit bun covers and always had brand-new leg warmers in every color in the spectrum. Although we were friends by necessity, there was an ineluctable note of malice to our interactions, and I wasn't surprised that she was singling me out.

"I don't know," I answered honestly, taken off guard. With no telltale defensiveness to chip away at, Leonelle let it drop, but something changed in that instant: Other people had noticed what I was doing with my head—what my head was doing to me, really—and unless I could stop, more questions were sure to follow. Later, when it was just the two of us sitting on the big leather chairs in the reception area waiting for our moms, who were consistently late, I asked Cynthia if she had noticed my head. "You know, what Leonelle was saying," are the words I think I used; I'm quite sure I didn't say twitch.

"Yes," she answered tentatively, unsure whether I would be more pleased by placating or the truth. Cynthia was a suck-up. "You've been doing it for a while. But it doesn't look that weird or anything," she was quick to add.

"What does it look like?" I asked. "Show me." I don't know to this day why I asked; being imitated, even now, affectionately, by those who love me most, is like bleeding internally, whatever I may say at the time. Maybe unconsciously I wanted, just once, to see what I looked like twitching in the eyes of others, so I would be armed for future reactions, surprise attacks. Cynthia looked uncomfortable, but she obeyed, jerking her head to the side in the same motion I'd observed in the mirrors. She did it a couple of times. "Okay," I said. "Thanks. Now don't ever do it again."

Although after that day I did sometimes feel eyes on me during lulls in ballet class—I never twitched while I was dancing, only when I was standing around waiting to dance—the twitch, and the others that followed, didn't prove much of a source of tension between my friends and me that summer. It's easy to be distracted at that age, and hierarchy, in spite of its shifty nature, is everything to eight-year-old girls. I discovered one morning how to give myself hickeys on the insides of my elbows—not that I called them that or knew what they were—and showed everyone else during one of the breaks we were allowed in long summer classes. Competitive hickey-making kept us occupied—and distracted—for weeks, especially when our mothers started noticing our bruise-covered arms and decided we'd all contracted some horrible contagious blood disease.

Before long, of course, my mother *did* notice my tic, which had gradually stopped being interesting and had instead morphed into a major source of confusion and dismay. The tic had worsened, coming more often—making it harder to conceal from others—and more intensely, causing me pain: primarily in the form of headaches and a permanently stiff neck. I'd grown accustomed to its patterns and habits; it occurred most frequently when I was overtired or under stress. The motion was involuntary, although I had a certain amount of control over it, to the extent that I could postpone or suppress it by focusing all my powers of concentration if the situation urgently required—such as in front of Leonelle—but I couldn't make myself stop. Sometimes I would do it in public for stretches at a time, frenetically, when no one was looking, but I also did it alone in my bedroom, flopped on my bed with a stack of library books and Midnight, our sociable cat, completely relaxed.

One weekend afternoon, as we sat over soup and sandwiches at the butcher-block counter in our kitchen, I looked up to see my mother watching me. Although I hadn't been aware of it—sometimes a ticcing episode caused me to zone-out for a number of seconds and reemerge blinking like a newborn—I knew I'd been twitching my neck; I felt the residual tension in my shoulders, at the top of my spine—the faintest shadow of pain.

"What was that, Amo?" my mother asked, pseudocasually, and I knew she was concerned: She and Alison are the only people in the world who call me Amo, ever, and they both reserve it for special occasions, when they're feeling particularly affectionate, or worried. Without thinking twice, and holding my head excruciatingly still, I said clearly, "Oh, you mean my neck? I hurt it at ballet. We were learning a new routine, and I twisted it funny. Can I have an aspirin?" It was an explanation so logical I almost believed it myself, and we resumed eating, my mother's eyes on me, all my energy focused on my efforts to hold still under the firm but gentle scrutiny. The next day my mother brought home a heating pad with a soft green-checked cover meant to soothe my "pulled muscle," which I secretly used for years as a mini–electric blanket on especially cold nights, although I'd been forbidden to leave it plugged in when I was asleep.

Alison spotted the tic too and zoned in like a vulture as soon as she realized it was a sore spot, like any younger sibling thrilled to have discovered a weakness, however unusual or unprecedented. With all the strength I could muster I forced myself to ignore her exaggerated impressions and relentless taunts, sure of only one thing: If I gave in and fought back, coughed up the reaction she was looking for, or really any reaction at all, she'd report back to my parents, who would possibly take her seriously and probe deeper than I wanted them to. Either he beat her to it and noticed on his own, or she *did* tell my father, who usually waited in the reception area to drive me home from ballet, looking slightly uncomfortable surrounded by so much rampant femininity, so many little girls, so many chattering moms.

One humid evening, just when I'd finally mastered a grueling routine, I turned to see my father standing right there in the doorway of the dance studio, in the spot generally occupied by Leonelle's mother, whose chief preoccupation in life seemed to be watching Leonelle. I smiled, pleased by the unsolicited attention, but stopped when I noticed his face. His expression was unfamiliar but hard to mistake: disapproval, even mild disgust. I felt an actual chill, although the air was hot and thick and the strands of hair that had wrestled free of my bun were plastered uncomfortably to my damp pink forehead. He was silent as we walked down the long flight of stairs and into the parking lot; he remained so for the first few minutes of the short drive home. Finally, with genuine puzzlement, he said it, the words spilling forth uncensored: "What in the world were you doing with your head?" My stomach lurched, and I knew that I had to twitch again, right that second, or I'd explode; I'd learned not long after its initial appearance that holding back the twitch usually backfired and led to a later, much worse bout. It occurred to me how much I'd been straining to keep him from noticing, him especially, far more than my ballet friends with their short attention spans and mostly deferential attitudes, my no-nonsense mother whose least favorite personality trait is self-pity, and even the infamously loose cannon that is Alison.

My father was never disappointed in me; we were two of a kind: freckled basketball addicts in matching baseball caps, memorizers of Beach Boys lyrics, lovers of coffee ice cream in pale sugar cones, the only two awake late at night on road trips, while we talked for hours about his childhood summers in Atlantic City and the plane crash that killed Buddy Holly and the Celtics' latest draft pick, always over the faint constant purr of my mother and sister snoring in the safe dark haven of the car. In relation to me and my sister, my mother always called him "soft as a grape," and it was true; he was a notorious pushover whose reputation extended well beyond our immediate family; my cousins and even certain friends knew whom to ask when everyone else had said no.

I'd never seen that look on his face, heard that undercurrent of festering anger in his voice, let alone had it aimed squarely at me. I pretended to adjust the buckles on my sandals and released a pair of twitches as I leaned into the cave below the glove box, forcing myself to keep them small and contained. "It looks crazy when you do that," he continued, his forehead crinkling unnaturally, his voice strained and beseeching. "Do you know that it makes you look crazy?"

Crazy. This soon became my father's word of choice to describe anything that could be even loosely interpreted as a tic. Sometimes, when he told me I looked crazy and launched into an explanation of all the ways in which my tics would surely make me a social pariah, I repeated the word over and over again in my head until it lost all meaning and sounded like a long bumpy hiss. I had never known anyone personally who was crazy, or at least what I thought was crazy; I didn't think my father had either. When my mother took us into Boston or Cambridge for a doctor's appointment or a shopping day, I stared openly at the old woman who cackled merrily on the corner of Newbury and Dartmouth streets, the man in full military garb who pushed a loaded grocery cart up and down the thoroughfares of Harvard Square. They gave crazy a face, a voice, a reason for being in the first place, and what did they possibly have to do with me? Crazy was loud, crazy was homeless, crazy happened in the city, where life was fast-paced and hectic and people ignored each other as they lugged briefcases and babies around with equal distraction. Crazy didn't happen in postcard-perfect Sudbury, in my cozy, colonial house; crazy happened someplace else.

In my own defense, and to deflect attention from myself, I monitored my dad; two could play at calling names. It wasn't difficult, once I started, to identify peculiar behaviors on his part to be used in aggressive counterattack; in fact, in my extended family, he was generally considered to be the neurotic one. For one, he was obsessed with mowing the lawn. The routine had evolved over the years into a ritual the likes of which I wasn't yet personally familiar with: It entailed the wearing of a certain Dallas Cowboys baseball cap, the smoking of a certain brand of cigar from a stock that was kept in a certain spot in the backyard shed and dipped into only on lawn-mowing days, and a razor-sharp mowing style resulting in rows that if measured would have been millimeters off from each other at most. The lawn mowing got on my nerves; it always had. The process was so rigid, so methodical—and besides, it rendered him inaccessible for entire Saturdays for half of the year; he couldn't hear yelling from as close as ten feet away when he was fully immersed in a good mow. It was as if he'd been hypnotized.

How best to interfere with what seemed on the surface to be an ordinary, mundane chore in which he took maybe unusual pleasure, but who was to say that was wrong? Only I seemed to detect anything abnormal in the trance he entered when embarking on a mowing episode, even when the lawn was brown and parched and so shorn already that no flecks of grass flew out of the mower as he pushed it up and down, up and down, like a machine himself, if you thought about it, or watched him for long. To an innocent bystander, the mowing must have seemed a pleasant pastime. To me, the energy expended in canvassing each individual blade of grass with such intensity sucked every drop of pleasure from the mindless activity. It tired me to see it. One day, lying down by the pond where the ground was too damp for him to push the mower, and following his eerily parallel lines, it struck me with evil glee: my inroad. I ran up the hill and tapped him on the arm, startling him into recognition, reentrance to the world beyond the lawn.

"Dad," I said, when he'd resignedly turned off the motor. "It's about the dandelions. You can't kill them like this. They're flowers. I can't stand it any more." My father hated dandelions with a passion that belied his normal-guy-spending-the-day-in-the-yard disguise. He couldn't fool me. "I hate those dandelions," he muttered sometimes at dinner after a rain spell that multiplied the yellow puffballs overnight until they peppered the lawn on all four sides of the house, like bobbing buoys in a sea of ragged green.

"That's ridiculous," he said, raising his thick eyebrows over the tops of his glasses with suspicion. Paydirt. I could smell the fear—I'd struck botanical gold. "They're weeds."

"If you won't stop mowing them," I continued, "I'm going to pick them, so you can't kill them, and then I'm going to scatter the seeds all over the yard." In response, he restarted the mower.

That summer I became a crusader for the lowly dandelion with a passion that would have likely embarrassed it, had it known of my efforts. I made small, full bouquets and placed them around the house, in my bedroom, in particular, outside of my mother's jurisdiction. Dandelion bouquets, I was willing to admit, were not to everyone's taste. I blew the white seedheads all over the lawn in plain sight of my dad, in direct defiance too ludicrous to punish and impossible to forbid—or to monitor, although he tried, as the dandelions grew faster and thicker than ever before, threatening to take over the lawn. "Who's crazy now?" I thought with well-earned satisfaction, as he crouched in the middle of the yard in a light summer rain, yanking out dandelion plants by the roots, hurling them with venom into the wheelbarrow he'd bought expressly for the purpose.

Pennies were my father's other sworn enemy. I could see that he could barely stand to be in the same room with a penny, and to my genuine dismay (such a waste!), he actually threw them away, handfuls at a time, even after I told him to give them to me, insisted that discarding money like that was certainly crazier than anything I ever did. It was a well-documented fact that he couldn't drive a car with pennies in it, in his sight; on occasion I'd place one on the dashboard just out of his reach while he was driving, and without fail he'd pull off the road at the nearest opportunity and throw it out the window with a withering look at me and an unconscious sigh of relief. I began a collection, with a zeal that came all too naturally, that matched my father's for elimination, although the irony of our shared ferocity never occurred to me at the time. If he was bound and determined to eliminate all the pennies he could, I was equally bound and determined to rescue them. My collection grew steadily, and I filled lidless jam jars with pennies and stacked the jars under my desk, where their solidity, their presence and bulk, gave me satisfaction at a glance, especially when I retreated to my room to twitch in privacy, to escape my father's tired tirades. When I caught Alison pilfering coins for penny candy one day, I realized I had to devise a more organized system, so I began keeping count and recording the totals on small slips of paper I kept hidden in my room and checked periodically. I never used any of the pennies, or thought to put them in rolls and turn them into the bank for what would have been a sizable sum for a nine-year-old, although my father was perhaps the world's biggest customer of those little cardboard coin rolls and stored bags of them in the basement, where he kept a desk and his hundreds of files.

In this peerless opposition, it's not difficult to detect the origins of the quiet storm that was to crackle electrically between us for the next fifteen years. My father and I did not grow less alike in the ways we have always been similar, and we never stopped spending time together, even when he was so frustrated and ashamed that he couldn't look at me, and I was so disappointed and enraged that in such a fundamental way my greatest advocate had unequivocally let me down. A new element appeared with the onset of my first tic, a dissonant chord complicated by the fact that we both remained convinced for years it could be eliminated—and our relationship restored to its previous companionable state—if only the other would *listen,* just try to understand and to change. All efforts were futile on my part: No matter how many times and in how many ways I explained to my father that I could not make myself stop the head twitch—and all the other twitches that were soon to follow—he refused to give up his misguided faith in my ability to do, or not do, anything I wanted if I would just work a little bit harder at it. And although I couldn't prove it at the time, I knew he wasn't capable of shaming me into stillness; if he had been, trust me, I'd have been cured.

Our dining room became a war zone; at meals my father was a sniper, watching me with an eagle's eye as he talked, passed food, and ate, exploding as much as he was capable of it at any unorthodox move. "Your head's going to fall off if you don't cut that out!" was his favorite, if illogical, accusation, destined to become the theme song of my youth, as far as he, Alison, and I were concerned; he cut way down on the commentary in the presence of my mother. After the first few months, growing low on the energy such wrath and attentiveness required, he adopted what was a far more insidious approach: an appalled stare, eyebrows raised in amazement at my "willingness" to act like that in front of anyone, and a simultaneous slow shaking of the head from side to side, as if all the degeneracy in the world had been condensed into a four-foot package and was sitting across from him at the dinner table. Sometimes this was accompanied by a low-pitched "crazy," in a voice just soft enough to be out of my mother's earshot, just loud enough for me to hear, even as I defiantly turned my head and looked away.

Alison saw an opportunity, found in my father's uncharacteristic and strictly defined lack of sensitivity an opening for her to attack without customary interference or rebuke. As only a sibling can do, she went for the jugular, pointing out each and every twitch my father managed to miss, keeping him informed as to those that took place in his absence, making sure my cousins—who lived ten minutes up the road and were our best friends and constant companions—knew that as far as twitching went, it was open season on me. "Your head's going to fall off," she'd whisper, when my mother was out of range, or, in response to my teasing or cruelty: At least I'm not the one who's *crazy*.

My mother took another route entirely, but not one that made mealtimes—or home life in general—any more pleasant. She was so angry with my father, for what she saw as humiliation tactics and poor parenting, that I took my rare moments of respite, during which I could wolf down food free from scrutiny, while she lectured him and quoted statistics from the educational journals that littered our house like groundcover, about how every glare, stare, and eye-roll was only making "the situation" worse. In private, she tried to wheedle me into confessing something; I wasn't sure what or I would have offered it up with pleasure. Was everything going well at school? Was I having problems with any of my friends? Was I doing too much? Maybe I needed to cut down on ballet. I balked at this in particular; I loved ballet, and although I certainly wasn't aware of it then, it provided me with the physical release that often seems like the only truly effective antidote to the thousands of little tics and rituals that weigh me down as effectively as an iron suit.

Finally, under unbearable pressure from my father, and because my evasiveness about what was clearly not just a sore neck was starting to worry her, my mother took me into Boston for an early yearly checkup. Dr. Hubbell, the unflappable bear of a pediatrician who had known me since birth, examined me perfunctorily, handed me a lollipop, and reassured my mother that I was absolutely fine. In his deep, well-modulated voice, he explained that my "high metabolism" contributed to any excess "nervous energy" we may have been noticing. He said he'd been watching me closely and hadn't noticed anything out of the ordinary—here came the chuck on the chin I'd grown to hate and expect—and, as I smoothed out the crinkly paper under me on his examining table, I knew I was freezing my neck as best I could so he couldn't say there was anything wrong with me. My mother persisted, and he finally allowed that yes, I might have a "little nervous tic, extremely common in children my age, certainly nothing to worry about." As he hustled us out into the hallway, he told us to keep an eye on it and let him know if and when it really started to bother me. I'm not the one it's bothering, I wanted to scream, but instead I smiled my most fake serene smile at the nurse who sat at the reception desk, and she passed me another lollipop when my mother and Dr. Hubbell had their backs turned.

The winter I turned ten I was one of the two girls in my

ballet school selected to dance the role of Clara in the Boston Repertory Ballet company's *Nutcracker.* A publicity photo I found recently of me in full costume and stage makeup looks as if it was taken during an actual performance. My head is tilted dramatically to one side as if I am gazing in wonder at the pirouetting snow queen or the Sugar Plum Fairy's initial appearance in her bejeweled tutu and diamond tiara. In point of fact, at many points during the show I was required to adopt this exact tilt of the head and overwrought expression of awe; Alison used to make fun of me for it, and even as I protested that the wide eyes and coy stance were necessary for dramatic effect, I had to admit that the pose looked stupid close-up. But when I held up the photo, its edges curled with age, and examined it closely in the light, I shuddered. This particular picture, I could see clearly now, shot after a dress rehearsal on an abandoned stage, was not a pose at all, but rather some photographer's unknowing documentation of that first mysterious twitch.

TICS ARE LIKE sentences: simple, compound, or complex. My head twitch is simple. One jerk, a motion and its negation, the return to original position a part of the movement, like flicking a light switch on and off, or opening and then shutting a door. Many of my tics are simple, in fact, variations on the head twitch involving a shoulder, a wrist, the muscles in my side, a foot, or an eye. Sniffing and blinking, swallowing and tapping, these too have a sole essential arc: out, and then in, up, and then down, back, and then forth. But as we acquire language, we learn more and more sophisticated means of expression; nothing stays simple for long. A few days after school started that year (Mrs. Egginson, third grade), a girl in my class whose hair seemed naturally to assume the feathered flip that all the cool third- and fourth-grade girls were wearing asked me out of the blue if I needed glasses.

"Why?" I asked. I had perfect eyesight, and third grade is young for glasses; I don't remember any of my friends having them yet.

"Your eyes," she said with a toss of her hair. "They're weird sometimes. Just forget it."

I knew what she was talking about then, and my face felt hot. Not only was my head still twitching, sometimes when it jerked to the side my eyes rolled up and out in the opposite direction. The twitch was getting worse. Maybe, I decided, I did need glasses, or at least I could say I was going to get them if anyone else asked me about my eyes. Although nobody did right away, fear of it happening made me shy, and I started to find reasons to stay indoors at recess, when the whole third grade would surely have enough time on their collective hands to notice that I'd turned into a freak, the kind of kid I would have made fun of myself just months before.

At home my father and I settled into a routine, unpleasant but tolerable, that amounted to an unhealthy stalemate. I could not stop twitching, especially at meals, when I knew I was being watched. I'd twitch, he'd stare and sigh, or even mimic me, which stung far more than I ever let on. After a twitching episode, my eyes inevitably turned to him, as if to the scene of a brutal bloody car crash, and he'd angle his head exaggeratedly to the side as if to say: See, this is what it looks like, it looks *this* bad. Often an imitation was followed by the old standby: "Your head's going to fall off," or the equally practiced sigh of disgust; the process became a vicious circle, as the anxiety his reaction provoked worsened rather than alleviated the tics, which I knew even at my angriest was his genuine intention. When I could muster the bravado, I'd tell him he was being an insensitive jerk, which he knew; he said so himself sometimes, when I *wasn't* twitching, but claimed that he "couldn't help it," an expression that strikes me as revelatory in retrospect. In the moment, though, he'd say, "Don't speak to your father like that," my mother, ever the teacher, would reprimand him for starting up in the first place, and we'd all simmer down until the next twitch.

At school, however, where most kids hadn't noticed my new "habit," I became consumed with trying not to twitch. The very idea of looking weird in front of the other kids was enough to send me to the girl's room up to ten times a day, where I could twitch all I wanted in private. I learned to go at odd times so Mrs. Egginson wouldn't grow aware of the frequency: at recess, during gym, in the bus line, when we had library hour or music. I didn't have ballet as much during the school year, but I hit upon other ways to harness energy during the newly interminable hours of nine to three, many designed specifically to make it seem less unusual that I wasn't outside with my friends, building forts and playing Capture the Flag, two activities that had made me the queen of the playground in previous years.

Mrs. Egginson was old, and she liked girls who were quiet and well behaved. In an attempt to fit the mold, to fit any comprehensible mold, I offered to decorate the blackboards for her, and she said that sounded like a delightful idea, until she realized the scope of what I had in mind. I started on a rarely used board in the back of the classroom, drawing tiny flowers with intertwining stems on a patch about a foot square. That took up one morning's recess and the latter half of lunch. The next day I started up where I'd left off, and after a couple of weeks the entire blackboard was covered, had become a dusty yellow garden dripping chalk dust like pollen, drawing oohs and ahs from the other girls in the class and just as desirable disparaging comments from the boys.

The following week I planned to start on the larger side board, a more prominent space, likely to attract even more attention than the back board had, but more important, guaranteed to keep me inside—and off the chopping block—for another two weeks. Monday's recess finally rolled around, but when all the boys and most of the girls had filed out the door that opened directly onto the playground, Mrs. Egginson was standing there with three of my classmates, one of whom was Susan, the girl who'd asked me about my eyes. "You've got some helpers," Mrs. Egginson said cheerfully, with no knowledge whatsoever of the knife she'd just stabbed in my back. I gritted my teeth and assigned each girl a particular section of the board, but after a few minutes it was clear that this particular escape had come to an end. None of their flowers were right—mine each had six precisely drawn petals, evenly spaced around a perfect circle— and when I tried to explain the problem to them, going so far as to erase one girl's especially sloppy patch, she smacked me with an eraser, leaving a faint striped rectangle on my navy-blue sweater.

"You're not the boss," she cried, alerting Mrs. Egginson,

who rushed over to praise all the sections of flowers, even the messiest, as "different but each beautiful in its own way, like real flowers." I felt my head twisting and fought the urge but lost; Mrs. Egginson caught the tail end of the now two-part motion, saw my eyes rolled out, and in her eyes I saw mild alarm. When I could, I glared at her. This was all her fault—if only she'd just let well enough alone. The next day I went out for recess with everybody else, but I swung the whole time, counting the pumps of my legs, jumping off only when I'd reached sixty, although the bell had already rung and I was the last one back in the classroom.

Sixty became an important number that year, and although I didn't share its magical powers with anyone else, I started using it as a panacea for the burgeoning levels of anxiety I knew were directly related to my twitch. I didn't question the fact that suddenly certain numbers were good and others (all odd ones, for example) bad, because counting was so effective as a relaxation technique and only grew more so over time. Soon I was counting before I permitted myself to do almost anything—talk to other kids, cross the street, answer the telephone, change the channel on the TV, respond to a question in the classroom. Later, when I learned that many sufferers of obsessive-compulsive disorder use numbers and counting in this way, I remembered how they were like a drug at first, a true addiction, in that the more I counted, the more I needed to, until the counting became more important and time consuming than the activity or act it preceded.

Counting wasn't the only activity capable of lulling me into a period of relative peace. One afternoon, when my tics were as itchy and irritable as chicken pox and I'd spent the entire library hour in a corner with a thick book gripped in each hand to still my jerking arms, Mrs. Egginson announced we were going to start learning cursive. The ligaments in my hands jumped, and I looked around quickly to see if anyone was looking at me. Nobody was. I raised my hand and asked if I could read in the library, as I already knew cursive, but Mrs. Egginson made a small tight smile and told me she was quite sure my cursive could use a little practice. I didn't push it, but I couldn't imagine how my cursive could be any better—at home I went over my mother's notes to herself and corrected the letters; grown-ups took shortcuts, my mother explained wearily, when I pointed out that her *b*s and *y*s weren't made right, the way they were in my "How to Teach Yourself Cursive" book. "What's important is being understood," she said, but I disagreed; it seemed more important to me than almost anything that each letter exist as a stand-alone work of art, correctly and perfectly formed.

"We'll start with the capitals," Mrs. Egginson announced, as she distributed the sage-green lined paper we used to write stories and for spelling tests, and when the stack came to me, without having planned to I took a half-inch hunk instead of a single sheet like everyone else. She began writing loopy *A*s and *B*s on the blackboard, and on either side I heard the murmurs and heavy breathing of intense concentration. I started to write. Over the summer my mother had bought me the aforementioned workbook for cursive, and during the many hours I spent in my room alone, I'd taught myself the alphabet. I loved the physical act of writing, both plain straight letters and swirling cursive; it provided such an innocent, immediate opportunity to achieve perfection—letters, unlike most things, could be finished, controlled. Mrs. Egginson's voice faded into a comforting background hum, and I finished another row, *a* to *z*, capitals first, then lowercase. I formed the letters meticulously, erasing each *h* with a crooked back, an *o* that wasn't a flawless circle, wearing holes through the flimsy paper in my attempts to make my letters match the models I'd studied in my book. When I felt a tap on my shoulder I looked up with mild surprise into Mrs. Egginson's questioning face. I followed her eyes down to my desk, where a small stack of pages sat in the corner covered with rows of letters. I looked around. My neighbors were working in their math books. In fact, everyone at my desk cluster was working in their math book. Without a word, I made sure the edges of my stack lined up evenly and slid it into my desk in one fast swoop. I took out my math book too, then, and Mrs. Egginson retreated to her desk. My arm felt stiff, half asleep, and I shook it out hard when she bent down to pick up a pencil.

Math had its fair share of sticking points too. I couldn't always just answer a simple problem and move on to the next one; sometimes I would look at the numbers in 6×4 and have to say them in my head twenty-four times. I experienced a secret thrill when 10×6 or 12×5 came up on paper or out loud, taking the unforced sixty as a sign that all was well with the world. Certain numbers I didn't like to say, see, or even think; threes, for example, gave me pause, and when I had to write a three in my math book I'd draw a faint mirror image so I could tell myself it was really an eight. All that year, when I needed to escape into myself to stop ticcing, I played number games, adding sixes to six, for example, over and over again, until I feared attracting unwanted attention by virtue of my inward retreat.

When my mother told me I had the option of changing

schools for fourth grade, I surprised us both by saying I wanted to switch. Although I'd justifiably earned a reputation for being painfully resistant to change—I composed dozens of rhyming elegies when my first elementary school closed down—the idea of a fresh start, with new kids and teachers who'd never seen me twitching, held enormous appeal, not to mention my secret hope that a new environment would maybe in itself stop me from twitching at all. My new teacher was one of my parents' oldest friends, a woman who'd taught with my mother for years and had known me since the week I was born. I felt totally comfortable with her, to the extent I had to remember to call her Miss Cushing and not Carol in school, and it didn't seem strange to her in the slightest when I volunteered to help her when I finished my assignments early, or asked if I could spend free time in the library; she'd been around when I'd learned how to read.

After school that year, I would often go to Julie's or Samantha's house, where I tried to twitch only when I thought it wouldn't be noticed, especially if any parents were around. Julie had a tree house, and one afternoon close to the end of the school year, the three of us were up there playing school. As usual, I was the teacher; as the oldest of the nine cousins on my mother's side of the family—all of whom grew up in the same town—I was accustomed to being in charge and assumed a mantle of authority as effort-lessly as I slipped on costumes from a dress-up chest, and with just as much pleasure. This game was off, though, and I wasn't sure why. Julie and Samantha had been acting strangely all afternoon, giggling and whispering to each other, and I was feeling left out. "Excuse me, teacher?" Samantha raised her hand.

"Yes, what is it?" I asked haughtily, trying not to sound insecure. I was grading worksheets in the far corner of the room and twitching a little bit; Julie and Samantha had seen me do it before—we spent enough time together that it was unavoidable—but we'd never discussed it outright.

"Julie and I (more giggling) would like to know why our teacher is acting like Johnny Hull."

My cheeks blazed; rare tears welled up in my eyes. Johnny was a boy in our town who had Down's syndrome and was being "mainstreamed" into the public schools; kids I knew didn't make fun of him to his face, but no one went out of their way to be nice either. He had four fingers on each hand, and his hands sometimes jerked out to the sides, like mine did once in a while. The following year he was in my fifth-grade class and ran for room representative; I will never forget watching him attempt to make a campaign speech while the boys in the back of the room snickered and whispered and I sat frozen in my spot on the speckled carpet, horrified for a terrible instant that the object of their derision was me.

"Just shut up," I hissed finally through clenched teeth, and scurried down the tree-house ladder as fast as I could, running into Julie's kitchen where I called my mom and insisted I had to come home right then.

"What's wrong, honey?" Julie's mom asked, from the table, where she was doing the crossword from *People* magazine. "Is everything okay?" Unable to speak for fear of releasing the tears, I nodded and went outside on the front steps to wait. The next day in school Julie and Samantha were solicitous and friendly, but the school year ended soon after, and our threesome fizzled out over the summer. That fall, whenever I saw Johnny Hull in the halls, I went out of my way to smile at him. Then I walked straight to the nearest girl's room where I could rock and tic until I managed to forget I'd ever seen him in the first place.

three

PASSING *for* NORMAL

My classmates at Nashoba, the all-girls' private school Alison and I started at when I was eleven, were, with few conspicuous exceptions, white, Protestant, and rich, updated Norman Rockwell kids with pedigrees and inbred politesse. They were far more homogenous than the kids in the Sudbury public schools, which were hardly bastions of diversity themselves; Johnny Hull would have stood out like a leper in this pristine environment and, after grilling me on the names of my new friends, my Bubby, my father's mother, told me not to forget where I came from. At the time I thought she meant Sudbury. Although the girls in my class were extraordinarily concerned with appearances—clothes, hair, cars, and even houses and furniture (many had met with interior decorators to design their own bedrooms)—they were surprisingly less judgmental than my former classmates and much more appreciative of what were perceived as my appealing, and though they would not have said this—or been aware of it on a conscious level—refreshing quirks. My parents, I think, were a little surprised by my new cadre of blond, boy-crazy, label-conscious friends, who laughed at everything I said and imitated my compulsive behaviors in an admiring, flattering way, without so much as a hint of degradation or mockery.

We had more freedom at Nashoba, where the classes were small and the expectations high, and sometimes a teacher would even leave a classroom for a little while, if we were in the middle of a test or a writing assignment. To my surprise, nobody took advantage of this, but kept working as if miniature video cameras were installed in the four corners of the ceiling. We were writing poems, I think, when I noticed that Abby, who sat next to me in English, was watching me write, not reading the words but absorbing the shapes of the letters, copying them in the air with her shiny pink pencil. For a few seconds I kept writing, ignoring her, until my pencil jerked on a letter and the irrepressible urge rose to erase it and fix it. Was that noticeably strange? Would she comment if I did it anyway? The risk was too great; I knew from experience that the erasing/revising process could consume five minutes, even more. That *was* strange, I was forced to acknowledge. I gripped my pencil so hard the pale blue veins on the back of my hand stood out in stark relief.

"What?" I said, without turning to face her. I pressed the tip of my pencil into the exact center of a period on the page, pressing down so hard the tip broke off. I pushed the bit of lead into the center of the period with the remaining stub. Then I sat back and met her eyes head-on. "Why are you staring at me?"

"I love your handwriting," she said. "It's so cool. Will you show me how?"

"It's just writing," I mumbled, embarrassed but pleased too; Abby was not prone to fawning, and her attention was universally coveted. I wrote out the cursive alphabet for her on an index card, as I'd memorized it years before, memorized it so hard and so thoroughly that my pencil flew across the page when I wrote longhand; only rarely these days did I slip up, forcing me to erase and rewrite, as I'd resisted this time, with Herculean effort and not a small amount of anxiety. Later that day, during the minor chaos of a science lab, Abby's best friend asked me if I'd make her a card too, and by the end of the day my hand was tired from making so many alphabet cards. The next day girls from other grades asked me to write their names on the covers of their notebooks, in cursive, in italics, with Magic Markers they thrust at me, placed in my hand. Somewhere in the back of my mind this bothered me, not writing the cards or the names, but the pleasure my friends took in writing their letters my way, when most of the time there was little pleasure in the process for me. By this point, writing out the alphabet, in different sizes, styles, and colors, consumed hours of my life each week and often hindered my ability to finish, or even start, my homework.

Very quickly, I became gratifyingly popular. All of my new friends' parents loved me; I was smart, well behaved, and able to converse with them on subjects they considered adult, such as current events and popular fiction. One friend's mother in particular took a liking to me and used to tell her daughter, my friend, to "keep moving all the time, like Amy does, that's how she stays so skinny." By this point finger- and toe-tapping were part of my rapidly expanding repertoire, and my inability to sit still attracted far more attention than my tics, especially from teachers—who told my parents I was a distraction to less-able students in class and made me sit away from the crowd, alone, in all classes held in circles on the rug. This lent me a certain dangerous quality that only added to my appeal.

It was at Nashoba that I learned to harness my tics and compulsions, conceived and perfected ways of concealing them as socially acceptable, if odd, behaviors. Tiny shoots of legitimate personality traits or characteristics—being hyperactive, a show-off, a know-it-all, a fidgeter, a slob—watered by the seductive attention of my peers, who interpreted oddness as renegade rebellion, obsession as identifiable style, became certifiable identity markers, clear-cut indications that I was me, even as I grew increasingly less sure who that was. Sometimes I felt as if I were creating a false bold self around my tics, like armor, a shell so watertight and impenetrable that my real self, trapped inside, rattled against the walls in faintest protest like seeds in a long-dried gourd.

Years later, when I was living in New York with Caitlin, the one friend I'd made at Nashoba with whom I stayed in touch, I asked her what she remembered about my tics from our childhood, when we'd spent hours together in the classroom and at each other's homes, on buses into Boston, at elaborate birthday parties all over the state of Massachusetts and beyond. She remembered some of the same things I did—the head twitch and the rolling eyes—and others I had forgotten: the way I used to go over the straight edges of my letters and numbers with my right thumbnail, a tendency I revert to these days only when signing my name, and the hoarding that began in preadolescence, when the contents of my desk spilled out into the rest of the classroom and even the hallway, and got incrementally worse over the following years.

"What did you make of it all," I asked, secretly appalled by her detailed recall, "especially the tics?"

"Well," she answered—we were roommates when I first received my diagnosis, and she was there when I started treatment—"I guess I thought what everyone thought. That they were just cool things that you did." At the time, I was glad of this assessment, relieved that I would be remembered by those with whom I'd fallen out of touch as "cool" and even worth imitating, rather than how I'd perceived myself as a preteen: as an imposter, a would-be empress in the proverbial new clothes. But later, when it sank in and spread, I remembered the section in my college psychology textbook that described how we are so conditioned to accepting what we see at face value that only enormous signposts make most of us note anything out of the ordinary.

PEOPLE SEE WHAT THEY WANT TO SEE, process the world around them in ways that make sense. Most people interpret my tics as signs of physical discomfort or ordinary stretching, even when they are extreme, or after I say no, I have not thrown out my back, slept funny, or acquired a crick in my neck. For as long as I can remember I have coexisted with an astonishing number of tics. Since that first head twitch, my tics have manifested themselves in a variety of ways, both physical and vocal, simple and elaborate, easily detectable—if you know what to look for—and easy to conceal. Sometimes one continues for years at a time, other times it lasts for just a few weeks before disappearing as unobtrusively as it arrived. I cannot predict what motions will or will not become tics; when I have a bad cold and am congested, my sniffing does not turn into a tic over time, for example. And although I've tried to pinpoint the arrival of various tics, I've never been able to do it, and will just realize one day that I am suddenly jutting out my chin or elbow for no apparent reason. Tics are sneaky; sometimes I don't even realize I've acquired a new one until Ben or Caroline points it out to me. Each tic has recurred at least once, but in no particular or predictable order.

Over the past twenty years I have tilted my head sideways to varying degrees—as first noticed in those unforgiving mirrors at ballet—thrust my chin forward, shifted my lower jaw to either side or back and forth, rolled my eyes to their outer corners, clicked my back or front teeth in patterns, and rotated my shoulder blades, as if I were trying to make them meet in the middle of my back. I have ground my teeth, tapped my thumbs against each of my fingers, cleared my throat, inhaled air through my nose in furtive little rabbit sniffs, snapped my jaw until it cracked, made clucking sounds in the back of my throat, hummed, emitted high-pitched squeals, repeated words and phrases that are said to me, and asked repetitive rhetorical questions unceasingly until I wear listeners into giving me some kind of a response. I bite my cuticles fiercely, methodically, until my fingers all bleed at the edges of the nails and crust over, at which point I gnaw on the dried blood and squeeze my fingertips to release more blood, to make more scabs, to ensure I'll have something left to gnaw. Whether I am listening to music or not my leg swings as if it, and not I, heard a beat. Sometimes my leg—or certain muscles in my shoulder blades—twitch without my noticing until I feel a pinch and check in a mirror for confirmation or just to watch them jump. My feet tap, usually alone but sometimes in sync, sometimes toes to the ground, sometimes heels. My hands angle out from my wrists in contained jerks, or clench in fists that look still but ever so slightly pulse in sequences.

The way I think is also a kind of tic but harder to sort into categories. It has to do with balance, with the evening out of lefts and rights, rights and wrongs, likes and dislikes. It entails excruciating attention to symmetry and making sure that everything "feels right," not perfect or tidy, but just whatever way it "has to be" at a given moment to set me at ease. If I see a face in a photo, painting, or illustration, I have to look at both sides equally, first the left, then the right, then both together, merged finally into a recognizable assemblage of features and shapes. If I see something out of the corner of my left eye, such as a leaf falling from a tree, I have to "balance" it by seeing something out of the corner of my right; sometimes I have to wait until another leaf falls so I can watch it with my right eye, even if it takes five full minutes, and I am running late.

People ask me all the time now how I lived for so long with all of these tics without being diagnosed or, more to the point, without insisting on a diagnosis. I always hear in these questions an implied accusation, geared more toward my parents than me, that surprises me still. When I look back on my childhood, after I started to have tics and before, when I was already showing signs of obsessive-compulsive disorder, this accusation never occurs to me. Partly because my memory is as compulsive as the rest of me and I catalog my experiences in the same way I catalog everything else, I remember vividly the frustration of being literally unable to control my body, the days when achieving control over my surroundings was tantamount to my ability to function from one minute to the next. But what I remember even more distinctly than the incidents of cruelty and confusion, intolerance and avoidance—more vividly than standing in front of the mirror watching my head move with no conscious instruction from me—is the strain of trying to conceal my tics and rituals from others, especially those closest to me, my own family most of all.

According to an article on the influence of gender in comorbid obsessive-compulsive disorder published by the American Academy of Child and Adolescent Psychiatry, it is not unusual that teachers failed to recognize my classic symptoms of Tourette's. The authors write, "It may be that in the classroom setting, the more disruptive behavior of affected boys is identified as aberrant, whereas the quiet involvement of affected girls in ritualistic or repetitive behaviors is overlooked. It is also possible that girls, who are more likely to experience a sensory precursor to tics, are likely to be more successful than boys in suppressing tics for periods of time, once tics are perceived as being socially disadvantageous." A few months after learning about my diagnosis, my mother told me something she'd kept to herself for years— my first-grade teacher had apparently sent home a report noting that she'd "never encountered a child with as many nervous habits as Amy Wilensky." After considerable agonizing, my mother confessed, she'd called my teacher, also her colleague and friend, and requested that the line be struck from my record; she didn't want me to be stigmatized in that way for the many teachers who were to follow.

I was reading before I was three, was dressed impeccably by my mother, who tied matching grosgrain ribbons in our glossy braids each morning and designed elaborate school bags to go with our picture-perfect jumpers and kilts, was just outgoing enough to avoid being labeled shy or introverted, was the kind of kid teachers always chose to run errands to the principal's office but who was never too pleased by the fact to invite the rejection of my peers. If ever a child was sent out into the world as trouble-free, it was me. It does seem odd to me in retrospect that *I* wasn't more curious about what my tics were and where they had come from; my pediatrician—whom I saw until I was eighteen and left for college—continued to use the expression "nervous tic," which sounds so general to me now, so unsatisfying, incomplete. We accepted what he said because it was easier than questioning, safer than what we might discover if we really searched. So I was "nervous" by temperament, a perfectionist held up to impossibly high standards by my teachers, parents, and younger sister, and therefore I ticced; when I learned to "better deal with stress," my tics would stop. I had an "unusually fast metabolism" that explained my inability to sit still, even for a few seconds at a time, and my manic energy; if I could establish regular sleep patterns and a well-balanced diet I would finally be able to "just relax." Whenever I heard this, I tried not to wonder too much why other "nervous" people, my father, for one, who spent virtually every waking moment in a state of near panic, did not have tics too.

It has not been until very recently that I have begun to

let go of what I remember most about growing up with tics: my conviction that they were mistakes I was making, outward signs of an inward lack of control, certainly not anyone else's business or responsibility. In short: my problem, my weakness, my fault.

four

THE BODY/MIND CONNECTION, *or* LACK THEREOF

In eighth grade, my very senses failed me, touch in particular. I lost my footing on sensation itself, and twisted comfort came only in several inexplicable phases involving clothing, including wearing a wool hat with a pompom that my grandmother knitted for me for nearly the entire month of October, which had been unseasonably warm—in the seventies, and sunny like July. At first it was assumed—even by me—to be an attention-getting scheme, but after a few days, when my friends tired of the novelty and I developed an itchy rash on my forehead, I came to terms with the reality of the situation: I could not remove the hat. I tried to explain this to one of my friends, the paralyzing fear that overcame me at the mere thought of taking it off my head, but she laughed and yanked it, waving it out of my reach for a joke. When she turned and saw my face, though, she thrust it back, mumbling an apology, which I quickly accepted: Had I been found out? One day, thank God, I woke up and didn't have to be wearing it, had lost in the night the need to have it pulled snug over my forehead, protecting my head from the sky, so I left it at home, where it sat in the coat closet with the rest of our winter garb, until it was actually cold.

I did lots of things I couldn't explain then, many of which went unnoticed, but some of which inevitably seeped through the cracks in the self I presented to others. I didn't mind being considered eccentric, depended on it, actually, as an alibi, but the line between odd and socially unacceptable is black and unwavering, and increasingly I was standing with both feet firmly planted on the wrong side. The summer before high school I wore my bathing suit twenty-four hours a day, swimming, showering, bathing, and even sleeping in it. After a few days my mother noticed and asked me about it, but I said I just wanted to be ready if anyone wanted to go swimming, which didn't sound too strange at first because my grandmother, who lived just up the street, had a swimming pool. When she pressed, days later, with a speech about the importance of cleanliness, I lied again, said I'd washed the suit myself in the sink several times, but felt secretly ashamed and decided to take it off once and for all that evening before going to bed. When nightfall came, however, after a tense, interminable afternoon, I couldn't do it; removing the bathing suit would lead to disaster, shatter the illusion of safety it represented, although I knew even through the relentless anxiety that this was not just illogical but ridiculous.

When I started to develop breasts I didn't get all excited and beg my mother to take me bra shopping like my classmates, who discussed the subject endlessly at recess and lunch and in the locker room getting ready for after-school sports. Underwire? Maidenform? Racerback? These words said nothing to me, could have been gibberish for all my response. While my friends batted terminology about with ill-fitting womanly delight, I composed chants in my head ("I am the same" is one that has stuck with me) with the intent of preventing me from undergoing the physical changes that accompany the process of growing up. To say I composed these chants is not exactly accurate; rather, I found myself saying them in my head, when the thought of being any different than I was at that moment in time seemed intolerable, and kept on doing so whenever I felt anxious or was fighting a tic.

Some of the chants weren't words or sentences but combinations of letters or numbers; the most common one, which I "used" over and over in a variety of situations, was to count from one to six and back, which I considered an equally powerful but less time-consuming relation to counting to sixty. Sometimes I said the numbers—or the other chants—so many times in my head that the act of doing so consumed big chunks of the day, leaving me disoriented and, in clear moments, furious with myself. When the chanting became nearly omnipresent, such as when I got my period shortly after turning fourteen, I wondered half seriously if I might have multiple personalities, like Sybil, whom I had read about with disturbing fascination. My two personalities, however, had the same name and were exactly alike, except for their differing views on the effectiveness of all of the activities designed to protect me from the formless fears that surrounded me like heavy fog.

As I got older, the tics got worse, not so much in frequency but in their very nature. They seemed to come from nowhere, multiply and feed off each other, diversify, rendering me unable to fend them off or package them neatly in categories, as I'd been able to do with my head twitch and its successor, the head/eye combination. Sometimes I wasn't sure what was a tic and what wasn't; I remember on the first day of high school when a blue-haired multipierced senior led us through what were called "the pits," basement rooms lined with cubbies for underclassmen to store books and belongings, and feeling as if I had to touch the right edge of each cubby in the bottom rows as we walked from room to room, unable to stop even as I lagged behind the group, terrified to draw attention to myself. This touching wasn't a tic, exactly, like my head twitch, but it wasn't voluntary either; it was a compulsion, preferable to my tics, in a way, because it fell under the umbrella of comprehensible behavior and I could pretend that I wanted to do it instead of had to, a distinction that meant everything to me, then and now. I didn't analyze my compulsions too closely; it was becoming so important to follow through on the instructions the crazy half of my mind was sending me, no matter how they looked to other people, that I paid less and less heed to the sane half, which kept insisting that the repetitive motions weren't remotely capable of fending off bad luck or worse.

My high school, Concord Academy, was an excellent place for me, in that its remarkable community of confident misfits and serious-minded free spirits allowed me to tic and carry out my increasingly bizarre behaviors largely unnoticed, or at least far less conspicuously than would have been the case in a more homogenous setting. When as an eighth-grader my parents dragged me around to different prep schools in the Boston area for tours and interviews, I walked across one impossibly green expanse of lawn after another inwardly shuddering, picturing how out of place I would feel, if not look, among these shiny, storybook teenagers with shining swinging hair and smooth, poreless faces, their lean obedient limbs. Although on the surface I was an ordinary suburban kid, probably indistinguishable from the ones I saw walking around holding lacrosse sticks like miniature, preppy Statues of Liberty, I envisioned myself standing alone in the middle of a manicured playing field in my shopworn bathing suit and grimy wool hat, never sufficiently comfortable in my skin, let alone my clothing, to hold still and act normal—let alone supernormal, which is, of course, the ideal status at most New England prep schools.

Socially, where I could pick and choose my companions, avoiding likely trouble spots, high school was less of a minefield than academics, with a few telling exceptions. I became acclimated early on to decanters and bottles and glasses with skinny stems that snapped when jostled too much in the sink. I'd mixed my first gin-and-tonics as a ten year old, with an expert twist of lime, and wasn't as caught up in the excitement of illicit drinking as some of my classmates were, especially the boarding students, for whom drinking in the dorms had the added attraction of outright defiance of the school's rules. When my friends started drinking, I realized I was going to have to take a public stand, one way or the other; one thing was for sure—if I abstained entirely, I would be a loser. I had always associated drinking with an upsetting loss of control—the way it made certain of my relatives act totally unlike themselves and do and say things I knew they wouldn't do or say when sober. For me, loss of control represented all of the ways in which my body was betraying me, changing me from an extrovert who liked to be the center of attention into a hunched form huddled in a bathroom stall for hours at a time, a dancer whose greatest source of pride had been mastery over her limbs to a broken-down robot, whose short circuits were causing a total system breakdown. Drinking would put the last shreds of control I maintained in jeopardy, leaving me dangerously vulnerable to the eyes of my friends, but I couldn't put it off forever.

One night in Harvard Square, I went to a Chinese restaurant with Monica, who was my best friend during school hours (as opposed to Caroline, who was my real best friend), partly because so many of her friends didn't go to Concord Academy and didn't have a larger context in which to place me. Monica had invited two boys I'd never met before along, friends of hers from Cambridge, and I felt pleasantly sophisticated to be eating out on a Friday night in the city, surrounded by college kids and real adults, none of whom gave us a second look. Halfway through the meal, Monica whispered that she needed me to come to the bathroom with her and to take my bag; I assumed she was hoping I had a tampon, so I was surprised when she grabbed her big shoulder bag too. I followed her anyway, and she pulled me into the handicapped stall, where she took a bottle of white wine out of her bag. "Just for us," she said, adding, "They've got their own," and I knew that this was a kind of a peer-approval test, providing me with a single acceptable option. It was cheap wine, thin and acrid, and it went down quickly; we finished in minutes, at which point Monica put the empty bottle in my bag and instructed me to deposit it on the street later, when no one was looking.

We ate the rest of our food fast and somewhat giddily, our voices loud and overly enthusiastic. I noticed obliquely that Monica and her friends seemed funnier and friendlier after the wine, but I was most aware of my own transformation. Whereas customarily the lines and angles of my body are sharply, distinctly drawn and experienced, it was as if they'd been ever so lightly erased, leaving behind a blurred, softer, far more pleasant version. I held out my hands and they felt boneless, as if the ligaments my piano teacher always noticed jumping had gently and painlessly dissolved; they were my hands, but then again they weren't: They felt rounded and lighter than air, as did my arms and shoulders and even my neck. I let my head roll in a circle, blissfully unaware that I was sitting at a table in the middle of a Chinese restaurant with three other people, savoring the sensation of having all of my parts working together so smoothly for once.

"Hey, what's going on over there?" one of Monica's friends said, looking at me with a kindly grin. "Someone can't handle her booze."

"No, she's fine," Monica said. "She's just enjoying it." And I was, but not quite in the way she meant. For years I had been so hyperaware of my body, so utterly conscious at all times of its inner twists and kinks, that it was a novelty to be granted an unexpected opportunity to revel in and then forget about it. After dinner, we walked up Massachusetts Avenue toward Monica's parents' house, laughing and shouting insults at Harvard students, stopping for rest on a bench outside the Square, where I spinelessly slid to the ground in a heap, still amazed by the luxury of somehow having let my hard exterior float off into the atmosphere like a noxious balloon. When we resumed walking, I was vaguely aware of forgetting something—maybe related to what my feet were supposed to be doing, or my hands?—but I couldn't quite get a handle on what, exactly, or locate the energy to worry about it. Later, just before passing out fully clothed in Monica's trundle bed, I realized that I'd walked a quarter of a mile without stepping on a single manhole cover, my most established walking ritual, or touching the fenceposts that lined the cemetery, or even counting my footsteps to make sure when I stopped that it was on an even number and preferably a multiple of six, which I did always, everywhere, regardless of companion or circumstance.

The next morning, when I woke up with a throbbing headache, I was consumed by a more pressing pain: the knowledge that I could well have done irrevocable damage by boldly and blatantly ignoring the strict rules that ensured my carefully guarded safety. Such reckless behavior all for the frivolous pleasure of a few tic-free hours! In a not-entirely conscious way, I'd begun to connect my tics with my rules and rituals, to view them as a sort of penance, wrapped up in the whole, complicated package that kept me from harm, as if I were my own deranged bodyguard or smothering spouse. Conveniently setting aside the real reason I'd chugged the wine—because not to have done so would have meant social jeopardy—I told myself it had been a lapse in judgment, an instructive episode to show me the pitfalls of escaping from myself, ironically the reason most teenagers, and adults too, drink—to "take the edge off," to feel comfortable when they would otherwise feel awkward, to slide away from reality, if only for a couple of hours. Growing up, the fact that my father did not drink, beyond an occasional sip of champagne for an unavoidable toast, was as accepted a reality as the fact that all of the other adults around me did. It wasn't until years later, when his sister told us that he was found passed out on the neighbor's front lawn the day after his high school graduation, that I wondered if he too had decided at some point that he was unwilling to loosen his tenuous but sustaining grasp on his self-control.

UNTIL HIGH SCHOOL, my adolescent experiences with boys had been limited to relatively innocent Friday night dances with Nashoba's "brother school" a couple of miles up the street. At Concord, many of my new friends were boys, with whom I could play poker and talk basketball and organize softball games at recess, but whenever any of my male friends so much as hinted at an interest beyond friendship, I slammed the door so forcefully on the possibility that it usually remained closed for good. Like drinking, sex had always represented to me a loss of control over the body, as well as representing an unthinkable connection with another person; now it also represented change of the most severe kind: growing up. There was the added complication of the fact that I almost couldn't stand to be touched, that even an inadvertent elbow in the ribs or a friendly hand on the shoulder threw off my sense of composure; Alison has complained since she could talk that I literally "wiped off" her—and all—kisses and in fact any contact of her or anyone's skin with mine—a much-appreciated result of my current medication has been a rediscovery of the pleasures of nonsexual physical contact with others, the ability to let others into my "personal space."

I had eventually conceded to hormones and stopped wrapping wide pieces of ribbon around my bony rib cage in a futile attempt to thwart my physical development. I had finally admitted to my mother and my closest friends that I had gotten my period, after a year of keeping it to myself, horrified by menstruation's ramifications—the onset of what I saw as a powerful system set irrevocably in motion for the next thirty to forty years. But I could not allow myself to act on the undeniable feelings I had for certain boys; once I did so, it seemed obvious, I would truly become an adult, a different person entirely, a creature guided by instinct instead of deliberate action and control. Fortunately, I was at a place where many of the other kids had their own reasons for abstaining from sustained sexual involvement or even a bare minimum of experimentation. It was still a high school, though, and there were plenty of exceptions to the rule.

One late-fall afternoon between soccer and basketball seasons, my friend Tim, who was older and could drive, and I set off for Burger King—a popular destination for day students with cars—for shakes and onion rings. We were parked in the day student parking lot chomping away in what I interpreted as companionable silence when Tim put his arm across the back of my seat. I stopped drinking my shake but kept the straw in my mouth to buy time; I recognized the nervousness emanating from Tim—as I tend to recognize anxiety in others, immediately, and with pervasive sympathy—but I was determined to deflect a situation sure to make me anxious and therefore likely to twitch. Tim was extremely popular, and I liked him a lot—liked knowing he liked me too, as more than a friend, if I was totally honest with myself—but that didn't mean I was ready to take an ir-reversible plunge. I noticed there were M&Ms on the floor of Tim's car, six of them, four brown, one yellow, one green, and this gave me strength; it was a sign: Everything would work out in the end.

"Look, Tim," I started, "I think we should—" Before I could finish, Tim leaned across the seat divider, crushing my onion rings to my chest, and kissed me full on the mouth. I kept my lips closed, but I was so taken aback that I didn't pull away immediately, just sat there, frozen, leaving Tim helpless to continue but too embarrassed to stop. After a few agonizing seconds, he gave up, sat back in his seat, and re-sumed eating his onion rings. I put mine back in the bag, "Tim," I began again, shaking a little but fighting the tics. I wasn't sure what I wanted to say, but I had already started counting to six and back in my head, to drown out the min-gled guilt and fear, and I knew I had to be alone soon where I could twitch. The yellow M&M, I observed in detach-ment, had been stepped on, was smooshed flat into the speckled floorpad, and I wondered why I hadn't noticed be-fore, how such a necessary detail had escaped me.

"Forget it," he said. "It's okay. Just forget it. Let's get out of here." I told Tim I had to pick up some stuff in my gym locker and we parted ways with mutual relief; I headed straight for the vacant shower stalls in the girl's locker room, where I knew I could twitch free from interruption. Stand-ing in the stall, I arranged my feet so my big toes were square in the center of two small pink floor tiles and twitched until I felt calm again; Tim called me that night to ask if I was mad at him, which surprised me, and I said no, of course not, but from that day on I avoided being alone in a car with a boy whenever possible. There were other boys, other close calls, but I was by then an expert at the art of creating and keeping distance, and I maintained flirtatious relationships over the telephone with one and then another, making arm's length a rule of thumb when it came to actual contact.

Unlike my friends and classmates, I had no time to swill vodka in the woods behind the gym and make out in the soundproof music rooms during free blocks and after school. My rituals and obsessions consumed all of my mental and physical energy. At the very end of my junior year, I woke up one morning after a week of being unusually tired with the worst sore throat I'd ever had. Shortly thereafter my mono spot test came back positive, launching a summer spent largely in bed. Once my throat felt better—and after the pneumonia I'd acquired thanks to my weakened immune system was gone—mono was more boring than painful and certainly undeserving of the time it consumed. In fact, after the first few weeks, when they'd tired of bringing me milkshakes and magazines and changing the channel on the TV my mom had moved into my room, my family was even more tired of it than I was and left me largely to my own devices. Instead of taking up a new language or, more realistically, catching up on the weeks of schoolwork I had missed (including my final exams), I became a full-fledged hypochondriac, upping the intensity level of my rituals to match.

The hypochondria began inconspicuously, in the guise of intellectual curiosity, as I read everything I could find at home or in the library about mononucleosis. It didn't matter that mono was relatively common among high school students and considered a relatively common and harmless virus. Its potential ensuing complications became a source of endless fascination for me, at least until I decided that the doctors were lying to me about my white blood cell count and that what I really had was leukemia. My grandfather had died a few years before from a heart attack caused by the radiation and chemotherapy treatments he'd undergone to fight lymphoma; that was my next self-diagnosis, after I'd circled microscopic bruises on my arms and legs with a ballpoint pen and tried in vain to get someone to take me to the doctor. For a brief period of time, when I caught a glimpse of my head in the hall mirror and thought it looked bigger than usual, it was encephalitis, but cancer—with its wide range of symptoms and hazy prognoses—was the disease that scared me the most. During my senior year I wrote a will, which I revised on a near-weekly basis, and composing good-bye letters and my funeral service—which I had planned down to the seating arrangements (my family, Caroline, Monica, and Kate in the front row) and the music (the Rolling Stones' "Ruby Tuesday" would play as my loved ones arrived in my backyard, where seats would be set up facing the pond) was a favorite pastime.

At night in my bed, where I spent hours trying to fall asleep, I imagined the mono coursing through my veins and destroying the healthy cells, one by one. I read in one of my aunt's medical books that the mono virus, once in your system, never leaves, but lies dormant for the rest of your life. I was sure it would not take much for those distorted mono cells to transform themselves into cancerous cells that would eat away at my organs until I was too sick to tell anybody what was wrong with me. Sometimes, even after I was healthy again, I thought I could feel the virus vibrating just under my skin, and I scratched my arms and calves until the top layer of skin flaked off and chapped patches stood out red against my pale, house-bound limbs.

While my parents were at work and my sister was at my grandmother's pool with my cousins, I busied myself establishing first-name familiarity with the pediatric doctors, nurses, and receptionists at Boston's Children's Hospital. Dr. Hubbell, who'd "diagnosed" my "nervous tic" all those years ago, was on sabbatical in Africa, and my new doctor, Dr. Goorin, liked me, I think, at first, and even admired my extensive knowledge when it came to blood diseases in general, and mono, lymphoma, and leukemia in particular. But after a week of fielding several questions a day from me ("If my gums look pale should I come in for another blood test? What does it mean if my eyelids feel heavy?") he finally set up an appointment. I looked pale and hollow-eyed after weeks cooped up indoors, but by this point I was perfectly healthy. I tried to gauge if my joints ached as we walked from the parking lot to the elevator, but I couldn't tell any more if I was just normal tired or cause-for-alarm tired, and I knew I wasn't going to get any sympathy from my mother, who distanced herself from my whining by telling me she'd be glad to drop me off at the inpatient ward across the street if I wanted to see some kids who were actually sick.

As I sat in the doctor's office pressing my finger pads to see if my nailbeds turned pink under the nails—one preliminary method of detecting a low white blood cell count— the doctor told me about his work with severely ill pediatric patients. He described the burn victim who'd lost most of his face and all of his fingers, a girl my age whose body had just rejected a bone marrow transplant, and another girl my age who'd died of leukemia just that week, holding the hand of her twin. Then he took both of my small hands in his rangy ones and told me I was a lucky girl, far too old to be wasting his, his staff's, and my own time in this way. He told me I was not sick anymore, did not have a terminal or other illness of any kind, and that he did not want to so much as hear my name until it came time for my next regular annual checkup. He forbade me to call him—or any other medical professional—unless I saw blood, and he meant it; I could hear it in his voice. I nodded, my cheeks flushing red, which I took as a reassuring sign that my red blood cell count was high. In spite of my embarrassment, it took years before I could say I was healthy and believe it, and I still do many of my health checks today, including daily pulse-taking and constant monitoring of my pupils; a lazy pupil, or one that does not change size according to the light, is one of the initial symptoms of a brain tumor.

MY SENIOR YEAR of high school my parents planned a family trip to Maui for us and my grandmother over Christmas vacation. I'd had a bad flight the previous year, when I'd accompanied Caroline and her family on what was a business trip to Honolulu for her father and a pleasure trip for the rest of us; somewhere over the Pacific Ocean, en route from Los Angeles, the plane ran into a bad patch of air, and the turbulence was unexpected and fierce. One instant we were sailing along so smoothly it didn't feel like we were moving at all; the next we dropped what seemed to me like thousands of feet, as if the cargo hold had been suddenly weighted with several tons of lead. Several of the babies on board started crying and shrieking. At one point the lights blinked off and on, and a stewardess stumbled in the aisle beside me; I saw fear in her eyes as she gripped my armrest to pull herself to her feet. The plane landed safely—we'd run into a storm—and Caroline's father, a seasoned traveler, assured us he'd flown through much bumpier skies. But that was it for me; I pledged never to set foot on a plane again, if I could help it, and entertained melodramatic fantasies of traveling the world by boat and train, in full-blown nineteenth-century dress, down to leather trunks for my extensive wardrobe and a wide-brimmed hat complete with scarf to keep the flecks of coal dust out of my eyes.

When the plans for the Maui trip were announced, although I'd flown dozens of other times over the course of my life without so much as a single pang of discomfort, that hour on the plane with Caroline came back to me magnified and grotesquely distorted. For weeks I lived in an alternate world, one in which my days were numbered, as there was no doubt in my mind that this trip—if I were forced to take it—would be my last. I spent hours each day imagining how the plane would fall, exactly: One engine would blow, and then another, and we'd career crazily down. The nose would hit first, killing the pilot and copilot instantly—splaying segments of their charred limbs about some unsuspecting neighborhood—and setting the front half of the plane on fire. The rear section would crash into the ground, splitting the plane in two, with such force that there would be no survivors, not a crying dog in the remnants of the cargo hold or a savvy stewardess who'd banked herself between two seats, no one at all. In fact, the bodies of the crew and passengers would never be identified because the flames would feed off the acrid-smelling fuel and blaze furiously for hours, burning every scrap of flesh and plane into fine, soft ash.

I thought, for a few days, that I had ESP or was clairvoyant; the plane crash I kept reliving in my waking nightmares had that vivid quality I imagined would accompany a premonition. I've rarely been as convinced of anything as that I was doomed to die in that plane. I offered to stay home by myself, told my parents—and meant it—that I'd rather walk to California in my bare feet and swim the Pacific Ocean than get on it. But my parents had little tolerance for my newfound fear of flying and even less for a child so spoiled as to be ungrateful for such an extravagant trip. I'd flown all over the world without so much as a peep, they pointed out and, as everyone kept telling me, flying was safer than driving a car, a tidbit of information that served primarily to render me also, for a while anyway, ill at ease on the road.

As the date of our departure neared, the rituals that had become an integral part of my daily routine tripled. Like fractals, old ones spawned new ones, especially designed to prevent the plane from crashing, to keep me alive until I'd landed safely back in Boston. At first, I was not allowed to touch any ground cover—floor, carpet, grass—with my bare feet. After a few days I amended this and decided I could not *have* bare feet, so I slept in my sneakers and socks; the sneakers were insurance. I washed my hair in the bathtub faucet and my body with a washcloth so I wouldn't have to shower or bathe with my shoes or socks on. Through it all, I twitched more than ever, as if I'd stuck my finger in an electrical socket and was holding it there. Then, one afternoon a week before we were scheduled to leave, when I was absentmindedly chewing a piece of gum, it struck me that chewing gum until the plane had landed safely would be another terrific insurance policy against a crash. For the next week I kept that same piece of gum in my mouth, tucking it between my gum and the inside of my cheek whenever I had to eat or drink. My counting rituals spiraled out of control; I remember eating spaghetti, pulling off two strands at a time from my tangled portion, convinced while I chewed that the even bites would surely keep me safe.

The truth is, even as I followed through with the most bizarre of these rituals—sweating in bed at night in my heavy wool socks, praying I wouldn't choke on my gum in my sleep—I wasn't truly convinced they would have the intended protective effect. Today, when I occasionally tap the threshold of my apartment door twice each time I leave and enter, I know more than ever how unconnected the ritual is with anything at all, let alone my personal safety or happiness or success. But obsessive-compulsive disorder, especially when it has something specific to focus on—such as a long flight—always drowns out the voice of doubt. Time after time I'm assaulted by the mythical devil on my shoulder, suggesting the absurd ritual to provide the relief, while the angel, speaking for my sanity, shouts faintly, as if from far away, "Don't do it! It doesn't make sense!" With the help of the angel voice ("What, are you going to stay home in Sudbury for the rest of your life?") I somehow made it on the plane to Maui, where the devil made himself a constant presence ("Do you really want to be personally responsible for the deaths of three hundred people?") and I forced myself to focus on the ancient wad of gum, hard as a pebble now in my aching mouth.

When the plane landed safely in Hawaii, I threw away my gum, having decided days before that this particular wad would work its spell only for the flight there—I'd have to acquire a new piece for the return trip. For the length of the ride to our hotel, I allowed myself to sit back, breathe deeply, and keep my mind a blank, increasingly the rarest of luxuries. Once I was settled in the bedroom Alison and I would be sharing for the week, however, the anxiety returned more intensely than ever. It was the week before my college applications were due, and although my father had done everything he could to speed up their completion, down to literally standing over me as I penciled in responses, he hadn't managed to nag me into writing the essay. The combination of the college application process—which had been doomed from the start, tic-wise, with its inevitable result of drastic life-altering change—with the impending return flight to Boston, ensured I was so tense I could barely carry on a conversation. The unfamiliar setting, another guaranteed tic inducer, was the final straw; the first day of the trip, as I sat on a stunning beach with my family under a ludicrously picturesque double rainbow, it became instantly clear to me: In order to protect myself and my family from a fatal crash on the return flight and to guarantee my acceptance at a desirable college, I had to touch wood.

I've always had to touch things. Sometimes I touch things I'm forbidden to touch; other times I touch things I'm allowed to touch but with no discernible purpose for the touching or in patterns that mark the touching as out of the ordinary. If a Wet Paint sign is in my vicinity, I'll have a spot of color on my right index finger, no matter how closely the freshly painted site is guarded, even if a rope barricades the painted surface. If a museum forbids visitors to touch the artwork, I'll risk triggering an alarm. Once I picked a ladyslipper—a flower that is endangered and therefore legally protected in Massachusetts—in the woods surrounding my grandparents' house, which I had been strictly forbidden to do. My mother was furious but bewildered—I was generally a kid who followed the rules, to the best of my ability anyway. I didn't even like the ladyslipper, I insisted, trying to give it to her, but I'd *had* to pick it.

When I read years later that Tourette's is considered a disorder of disinhibition, removing the barriers in its sufferers that keep most people from crossing certain boundaries, I immediately saw that ladyslipper wilting on a bed of pine needles where I'd made a sort of grave for it down by the mailbox; I'd had no desire to keep it, even after I'd been told that I could, that the damage had already been done. At ten I turned the alarm switch to "on" in my father's mother's bathroom at her assisted-living facility, as I'd been instructed not to do a thousand times. I remember that day too, standing in my Bubby's spotless pink-and-white bathroom alone, absorbing the sickeningly sweet smell of baby powder with every intake of breath, and just touching the tip of the switch, hoping it would be enough. It wasn't. When the police came, again I had nothing to say. A few years later I stepped outside a store at a mall holding a dress with a plastic security tag attached to it, knowing an alarm would go off, mortified at the thought of being mistaken for a shoplifter but unable to resist bringing it—and me—over the invisible line.

Sometimes I touch things that cause me pain, for the same reason: because my brain sends me a firm message to do so. I have often burned the tips of my fingers by touching stove burners (much in the same way I look directly at the sun until all I see is hot white light, even though I know this is asking for permanent eye damage in the form of burned retinas). I have pricked my fingertips with straight pins, not with quick jabs but slow deliberate pushes. Most of the time the touching goes unnoticed, is likely perceived as a casual swing of the arm, a meaningless brush against the unfeeling surface of an inanimate object. Racks of clothes in department stores are a favorite target, as are the vertical tips of fenceposts, books on a shelf, eggs in a carton, the fur collar on the coat of the woman in line in front of me at the bank. More often than not I touch in numbers; the numbers are always even, usually two, four, six, or even a multiple of six.

Somehow the wood was different—to begin with, I quickly stopped caring about being found out. It started as always on a small scale: a hand resting on a tabletop, two toothpicks pocketed at lunch, toe-tapping on the threshold and boards of the floor. Then one day these subtle touches weren't enough. I felt best—meaning calmest, safest—when I was touching wood all the time. I spent much of the vacation either sitting on the one wood-backed chair in our bedroom, when we were at the hotel, collecting twigs and scraps of bark to stuff in my pockets, dashing from tree to tree, anxious to reach the safety zone of a wooden trunk. Out for dinner one evening, I sank into my seat with relief when I saw the burnished hardwood table, sat gratefully throughout the meal with each forearm pressed firmly against its surface, indulging myself in the reassuring illusion that the wood itself was seeping into my eager pores.

The day before we flew home, we took a long drive, the

"Road to Hana," in our little gray rental car. I insisted on sitting in the middle of the backseat—between my grandmother and Alison—in the hope that being wedged between two immutable forces would keep me from succumbing to my urges, induce a forced period of rest. At first I was fine, soothed by the closeness of the warm bodies on either side of me, the soft, resisting upholstery of the car, and I looked straight ahead, at the road, so as not to be distracted by the taunting, ubiquitous trees. We parked at a waterfall for lunch, and I ate happily, having spotted a picnic table—wood, of course—on which we could spread out our food. I hadn't been twitching much at all—the wood touching expended so much energy it didn't leave much left over—and my father praised me for it and said, "You're keeping your head still," approvingly, which thrilled me, even though I knew I couldn't justifiably take credit for not twitching if I wouldn't accept blame for doing so.

When we piled back in the car for the final leg of the drive, however, as if to spite my good mood, the wood-touching urge returned without warning, seemingly having gathered strength in its absence. My hands were shaking, so I clasped them tightly together, then sat on them when the ligaments wouldn't stop twitching. In an effort to meet the urge halfway I started counting the trees, the ones closest to the road anyway, but at thirty-five miles per hour I couldn't keep up, and it seemed riskier—more likely to upset the OCD powers-that-be—to count inaccurately than to stop counting altogether. When I found myself planning a dramatic and possibly fatal roll onto the side of the road from the moving car, I gave in.

"Stop," I commanded, and when my father kept driving

I yelled it, causing my mother to turn and raise her eyebrows at me.

"Are you ill?" she asked, rolling down her window and then the other three. "Here's some fresh air."

"Yes," I said, "and I'm going to be sick if we don't stop right now." Alison leaned as far away from me as she could with undisguised disgust, and my grandmother felt my forehead with the cool dry back of her hand. I felt no guilt at the deception; the compulsion was so single-minded I couldn't assess it with any grasp on reality. Finally he pulled over, when a rare shoulder appeared on the narrow road, and I practically shoved Alison out of the car in my efforts to reach the closest tree. For a moment I stood there with my arms wrapped around it, hugging it, really, with tremendous relief. My family was stretching their legs and reorganizing the crowded car; no one commented on my newfound love of nature. Quickly I decided I had to touch as many trees in the area as I could before I was ushered back, though, and this did provoke a response.

"What the hell is she doing?" I heard my mother say, as I ran around like a chicken with its head cut off, slapping trunks with both hands, and I was actually glad she hadn't suspected my secret: my inability to stop myself. I was happy to be accused of "acting out" or "trying to get attention," if it meant concealing the truth.

"She's been weird for the whole trip," Alison said. My mother led me firmly back to the car.

We didn't discuss the wood touching, then or ever, and it is likely that, as per custom, it was dismissed as an isolated, inexplicable incident in my family's idealized version of me. Although for years I'd followed suit—when it came to me, mistakes were aberrations, insanity, when it reared its ugly head, was temporary—this piece seemed to belong to another puzzle entirely; I couldn't make it fit, no matter how hard I tried. For me, that week, and the vivid picture of the tree I'd embraced, represented a turning point. For the first time I allowed myself to acknowledge that my intrusive thoughts and subsequent compulsions interfered with my ability to function in a normal way. When I returned to school and my immutable daily routine, wood lost its hold on me, but for once the memory of the intensity of its pull failed to fade. I still had no words to describe the involuntary nature of the touching, but I'd irrevocably crossed into territory I'd been pretending not to see.

Before the end of high school, *L.A. Law,* one of the hit TV shows of the late '80s, aired an episode featuring a man who was suing his former employer for firing him based on the profane outbursts and jerking movements he claimed were not under his control, but rather symptoms of a disorder called Tourette's. I saw the show by myself, when I was supposed to be doing my homework, and as a hypochondriac was captivated by the descriptions of the disorder. It was the first time I'd ever heard of it, heard the word, even, and like the prosecution, I found it an intriguing defense— good entertainment—but ultimately hard to swallow. The next day the subject came up over lunch—everybody watched *L.A. Law*—and I was one of the more ardent disbelievers. Self-righteously, and without a twinge of disingenuousness, I argued that such ugly thoughts and movements could not be blamed on the brain alone; sufferers of this disorder must in some way, maybe unconsciously, not want to suppress them. Although the conversation petered out, with some of us speculating the disorder was fictional, had actually been invented by the writers for the purposes of the drama, it lingered with me in an inexplicable way. Sometimes I thought about that man, so coherent and intelligent when he wasn't in the midst of a Tourettic outburst, so unsightly and unrecognizable when he was, and felt somehow uneasy, as if I'd been quick to judge what I couldn't understand.

Concord's intellectual demands were impressive, and from day one my mind and body conspired to make the process of learning as much like pulling teeth as possible. When I had homework to do—or any task, such as the dishes or cleaning my room—unrelated, unnecessary minutiae washed over me like a tidal wave. Many of these time-filler activities were centered around grooming, which doesn't come naturally to me; left to my own devices I often forget to so much as brush my hair or pick clumps of cat hair off my holey sweaters and buttonless coats. The more I had to do, the more involved my rituals became; I clipped at and filed my nails for hours, removing every last trace of cuticle left in the wake of my incessant gnawing. I searched my hair for split ends, snipped them out when I found them, and counted them, not stopping until I removed a certain number, say sixty. Sometimes this required my breaking individual hairs to create a split end to cut off.

The most consuming practice, however, was inspecting and picking at my skin, which became a morning, afternoon, and evening obsession. In retrospect, from photographs, and as my parents and friends kept telling me then, for a teenager I had a relatively good complexion, with only an occasional innocuous blemish or spot. I rolled my eyes when people told me this; clearly, the lies were intended to spare my feelings—someone whose skin was as marred and repulsive as mine should not be allowed to subject others to it by walking around in public. I acquired a medicine cabinet full of skin-care products, spent all the money I had restocking it, and many pictures of me at home from my high school years show my face speckled with up to twenty white or green blobs of some new cream or gel. I wore cover-up products to conceal my imagined pimples and my real freckles and, on occasion, refused to leave the house when I fancied my skin looked especially bad. In the bathroom I shared with Alison I became a mad facialist, performing extractions at such length and of such severity that my eyes would water and my skin would bleed, further perpetuating the cycle of products and concealers. I scanned my face with a magnifying glass I'd found in a drawer in the kitchen and undertook frequent minor surgery—in the tricky dual role of surgeon and patient—with the help of open safety pins or needles I'd held in a flame for a few seconds to sterilize them.

There are still days I want to rip off my skin with my fingernails, have to interlock my fingers or sit on my hands to keep from making an initial gratifying gouge. I imagine my body as a skinned tomato, a raw, pulpy mass with no corners to knock against each other, no layers to prickle and nag. At these times, nothing sits right, not my hair or my clothes or my arms or my legs or my eyes or my voice or my brain. Texture itself irritates; I remember a wool sweater with reindeer on it that used to reduce me to tears as a child, I could so little tolerate the feel of it on my skin. Like me, Bryant recalls changing outfits dozens of times each morning on school days, complaining to his uncomprehending mother that "nothing felt right." Most people's brains censor such thoughts and feelings through an active process of inhibition; in those with Tourette's, this ability is impaired, causing tics—the only remedy at our limited disposal, the body's way of saying: This isn't working for me.

five ⸻⸻⸻⸻⸻⸻⸻⸻⸻⸻⸻⸻⸻⸻

THE WORSE
BEFORE *the* BETTER

At Concord, for the first time in my life, I wasn't one of a few smart students attracting favoritism from teachers and resentment or special treatment from other kids for being different: Almost everyone was smart, eccentricity was practically a requirement for admission, and as far as those around me were concerned, I was as remarkable and unremarkable as everybody else. Although I expected to find it easy to learn in a school where I didn't first and foremost feel out of place, it was apparent after just a few weeks that I was somehow incapable of the two basic requirements of higher academic success: taking notes and doing homework. In the fall of my freshman year my math teacher called my parents in for a conference. Later that evening over a typically tense dinner during which I struggled more than usual not to twitch, suspecting the forthcoming confrontation, my mother finally asked, "Can you please explain why you haven't turned in a single geometry assignment all term?"

I thought for a minute, really truly thought. Why *couldn't* I do my homework? Just the night before, I had sat down at my desk at 5:30 with a Coke and two freshly sharpened pencils, my assignments for the following day written in a neat column for a change. I sorted my textbooks in alphabetical order by subject: biology, English, French, geometry, history. Five subjects, but the odd number couldn't be legitimately revised—I wrote "snack" in neat block letters under "history," though, just to be safe. Then, I drew perfect little squares to the right of each assignment, to be checked off when the work was completed. I flipped through my biology book to the section on genetics and stared at the chart on the heredity of eye color, which we hadn't studied yet in class. I took a sheet of paper from my notebook and charted my own family's eye color progression, making a separate chart for my own two possible future scenarios: if I had a child someday with a blue-eyed man and if I had a child someday with a brown-eyed man. As I was wondering about the potential effect of a man with eyes that were gray or green, Alison yelled up the stairs that I had a phone call, and I ran into my parents' room, where the telephone sat on a nightstand, and spent an hour on the phone discussing the various merits and flaws of the blue- and brown-eyed boys in Concord Academy's student body, after which I decided I'd just take a quick bath before starting the biology assignment. By the time it was midnight, all I'd done was tear out sheets of notebook paper for each class' assignment and written my name, the date, and the subject neatly at the top of each page. I was so tired from the previous evening's like routine that I fell asleep reading a book that wasn't for school with the lights still on; when I woke up six hours later, I remembered that I had a quiz that day on a short story I hadn't read yet in English, and I spent the ride to school skimming it while my mother hummed along off-key to her Cat Stevens tape, ignorant to my distress.

I couldn't diagram this pattern for my mother, though; it sounded ridiculous. "I try to do it," I said finally, lamely, "but somehow I can't." I knew everyone thought I was lazy; I suspected it myself. My father, who lived by a digital clock that seemed to be implanted in his brain, bought me self-help books on getting organized and "conquering time," which as a concept was increasingly out of my grasp; if anything, I felt, time had me whipped into the ground. Both of my parents made rules, established an in-house study hall, during which I could not read, watch television, or talk on the phone, but I still couldn't get anything done; most of the time I couldn't even get started.

Geometry had fazed me, it was true: For the first time ever I had looked at a problem, not known the answer, and frozen up, largely due to the realization that the walk in the park that had been my education thus far was grinding to an unceremonious halt. But something other than simply finding my work challenging was going on in my head. Even in classes that weren't so hard, such as English and French, or for assignments I enjoyed—creative writing pieces or art projects—sitting down to begin anything had become impossible, and the stress I incurred from dealing with the ramifications—playing constant catch-up—was worsening my tics. In school I made excuses upon excuses for "lost" homework, and at home I stayed up all night before tests memorizing all the material I could. Most of the time I managed to scrape by, but each time I had to question if the struggle to acquire a reluctant classmate's notes, stay up all night committing formulas I didn't understand to memory, and bushwack through tests that might as well have been written in Arabic for all I recognized the questions was worth the passing grade.

When I look through my notebooks from these classes now, and you can be sure I have every single one of them, I am reminded of the movie *The Shining,* in which a writer played by Jack Nicholson spends a long, isolated winter supposedly finishing a novel. What he is really doing is typing up an entire manuscript, hundreds of pages, that consists of one repeated sentence: "All work and no play makes Jack a dull boy." Whenever I see this movie, my initial response to the scene in which this depravity is revealed is envy: Imagine the pride he must take in such glorious, zealous repetition! From the eight years I spent in high school and college I have about ten pages of legitimate notes, many of which are illegible due to the cursive alphabets spiraling over and around them. Ten pages total—over nearly a decade of what was intended to be a rigorous education. Being in class, trying to listen to the teacher over the voice in my head that was repeating words and numbers, watching the other kids record their assignments and take careful notes, felt surreal, as if I were ephemeral, residing in a parallel universe, one in which I saw full well what I was meant to be doing even as I knew I couldn't do it, lacked the necessary structures. I could step outside my enclosed world sometimes and see myself sitting at my desk, filling page after page with my name, which I liked to write in full, as the inclusion of my middle name—Suzanne—made the number of letters come out right, even as I registered that I was letting the lesson pass by unrecorded.

Sometimes out of sympathy I would get undeserved help—a summary of the class discussion, a suggestion for a paper topic, a loaned book that explained an obscure poem, a fancy calculator to use during the upcoming test. I passed off my lack of knowledge as disorganization, and the reputation I rapidly acquired as a slob and a flake propelled me through the rest of my years in school, explaining away the inexplicable, providing excuses for the inexcusable, nourishing the identity as a "character" I'd settled into at Nashoba and was still all too willing to assume. Friends, and then friends of friends, asked to see the contents of my backpack or notebook for entertainment, calling still more kids over to witness the display; one morning, to the delight of Caroline and a few other girls I didn't know that well, I pulled items from inside the lining of my coat one by one like a magician—the crowning glory was a half-full can of Pringles I'd forgotten I'd stashed there.

I liked feeling cocky when I did well on a test or a paper in spite of my lack of preparation and made a show of completing my work under the teacher's eye in class or during an assembly or all-school meeting. The truth was that during class, I was far too busy to record mundane details such as due dates and exam schedules, let alone the material we were studying at the time. I had to write the alphabet in cursive and calligraphy, hundreds of times on a page. I had to make elaborate crossword puzzles that worked, and write long words, such as "totalitarianism," at the top of a page, so I could make as many as possible small words (trains, malaria) out of the letters. I had to compose far-fetched to-do lists with unachievable goals, and calculate what my GPA would be if I managed to get a B- in biology without having done any of the out-of-class lab work.

The "distractions" were limitless, knew no decency, had no boundaries, as far as I could tell. Alphabetizing appealed immensely to my sense of order, and my bookshelves, record albums, and even the clothes in my closet were so meticulously organized in the days before I had a test or a research paper due that I noticed so much as a single borrowed novel or rumpled skirt, kept in the skirt category "p," for pleats. My father, whose exasperation with my problems completing my homework came close to matching his anguish over my increasingly frequent and unsightly tics, approved of this kind of order; his own possessions were equally well organized, and when he broke down and permitted me to borrow one of his many sweaters, he would open his sacred sweater closet, carefully slide out the requested sweater—folded shop-style in an individual Byford plastic sweater case—and hand it over to me as if it were made of handblown glass. When I returned it, even if I'd worn it for just a few hours, it would go straight off to the dry cleaner's and eventually get returned to its designated bag and precise location in the closet.

Although my father occasionally begrudgingly lent me a sweater, he was less and less able to understand my inability to follow even the loosest of guidelines, to live within any kind of a structure. One evening, as I sat devouring a cheeseburger with some of my boarding student friends in the dining hall, a senior I'd never spoken to before approached our table with palpable disdain.

"Are you Amy Wilensky?" she asked, examining her

nails, which were painted in what I thought a most sophisticated dragon-lady red.

"Yeah," I answered loudly, making sure everyone in the vicinity saw her talking to me. "Why?"

"Your father's walking around outside, over by the gym, looking for you."

"Thanks," I muttered, my voice now barely audible. I sensed compassion behind her smirk and from my dining companions; a campus-roaming, indiscriminately inquisitive parent was almost too obscene to imagine. The senior glided off, a flash of black swaddling and red talons, and I looked up at the clock on the wall. It was 6:00, and I'd promised that morning, absolutely sworn on my life, that I'd be out at Main Gate with all of my books by 5:30, when my father was scheduled to pick me up. I gulped down the last of the burger and sprinted full speed to my cubby, where I shoved random books in my bag, thrust one arm into my coat, and prayed that my father had returned to his car like a sane person, before he completely humiliated me in front of every cool senior in the school. I ran into him on my way to the car, where we both maintained a grim silence until we were seat-belted in with the doors slammed shut, as other, functional kids passed by on their way to their dorms or the library or slid into cars with their smiling, functional parents.

"Is my time worth anything to you?" he asked then, his eyebrows pointing up in the middle, and I settled in for the lecture, while I wondered nervously which other students he'd queried as to my whereabouts, tried to think of who would have been lurking around. Again, when he finished speaking, I promised that the next day, barring death or dismemberment, I would be sitting at the gate waiting for him at 5:30 sharp, but the promise sounded hollow even to me, and he just gripped the steering wheel harder, jaw clenched in residual anger, shaking his head. What I didn't say, didn't understand, was that I *had* tried to show up on time, at least up until the point I sat down in the cafeteria, my own home and our planned family dinner completely forgotten.

After soccer practice, I had forced myself to walk away from the pack of teammates headed over to the south field to watch the end of the boys' game in progress, kept my eyes on the gym door as I counted my steps, and walked in a straight line without stopping to talk to anyone along the way. I'd even condensed the rituals I usually performed in this given situation—picking up twigs and stones that caught my eye on the path, touching the tiles on the hall floor with my right toe and then my left as I walked to the locker room, running my hand along the lockers in my row six times—all slowed by the fact that they had to be performed without detection. This, too, wasn't worth explaining; how could I say that I was late because, first of all, I'd been counting in my head, and that, second of all, the counting had made me forget I was being picked up in the first place? I wasn't about to set myself up for the "crazy" lecture; I was all too happy to settle for the "lateness" one; I'd hear it again if I had to. Again and again and again.

My father and I had one safe subject throughout these years at-odds, a fallback as reliable as the passing of time. For many people, being a sports fan is a hobby. For a select few, it is a way of life, a veritable means of sustenance as necessary as vitamins and minerals, or water. Over the twenty-six years my dad has been a Boston Celtics season ticket holder, I have attended hundreds of games with him, starting when I was three and had to sit on a folded blanket to see over the permed red hair of the woman who sat in front of me with her rotating dates. Basketball—not just watching but playing it, every day at lunch, up to two nights a week, and on Sunday mornings—is a defining ritual for my father, and through him, it has become one for me.

"Game tonight," he reminded me when he woke me up for school one morning. "Seven-thirty start. I leave without you if you're not standing by the door, coat on, at five-thirty on the dot." Five-thirty is standard departure time for a 7:30 game; for games that begin later, or if we're having dinner downtown beforehand, he adjusts this, but it's always exceedingly early, factoring in overly generous leeway for traffic or other potentially delaying factors. We park in the same garage, in the same space; when the Boston Garden became the Fleet Center, we lost touch with Paul, a red-faced drunk who often forgot which cars were whose but who always saved the choicest spot right by the exit for my dad. We eat the same foods, bought at the same stands, served by the same men, who know both of our names. And we sit in the same seats—me on the left, my dad on the right—chewing our cuticles in unison during tense parts of the game.

During high school I went to games up to twice a week. The ritual of the evening—which never varied—encapsulated many smaller rituals for me. At one game, midseason of my sophomore year, I realized that I had developed a clapping routine. When a Celtic scored, I had to clap twelve times exactly: three times fast with my right hand over my left, three times fast with the left over the right, and then one full repetition of the cycle. When a critical regular basket or a daring three-pointer was scored, my clapping pattern went wholly unnoticed, as nearly fifteen thousand people leapt to their feet—this was the '80s, after all, and the Celtics were still the Celtics. But when Dennis Johnson hit an irrelevant free throw in a game we were winning by twenty points, and I clapped twelve times in virtual silence because I had to—a basket was a basket, no exceptions—people in our section, and my dad, turned and stared.

"What are you doing?" he whispered, making sure the people around us weren't staring at me, or at him.

"I'm just excited," I protested. "I love beating the Knicks." Truth? Sixes, and multiples of sixes, were by this point absolutely vital as a means of survival. Without being able to pinpoint when—or why—I had begun doing almost everything in sixes: brushing my teeth, six back-and-forth strokes on each quadrant of my mouth; taking steps—when a walk didn't naturally end on a multiple of six I would as unobtrusively as possible take the requisite number of steps in place to make up the difference. Even speaking—although I couldn't always think quickly enough, I got tremendous satisfaction from speaking in groups of six words at a time, and always made a point of saying "Hello, it's nice to meet you" upon being introduced to someone, concluding after some internal debate that contractions were technically only one word.

At the Celtics' games, in an enclosed space for a finite period of time with my father, in front of whom twitching—and especially twitching in public—was taboo, sixes were omnipotent. Besides the clapping, my cuticle chewing took on a manic quality, became rodentlike. I chewed deliberately six times at the edge of each nail throughout this entire game; the next day a friend from school, who'd been

seated in another section with his father, told me he'd identified me across the court when he spotted my hands at my
face, my nails darting in and out of my mouth. Also, as a genuine fan and a full-fledged competitor myself, I hated to see
the Celtics lose. Somehow my behaviors became wrapped
up in their successes and failures; although I knew that
whether I held my breath for twelve seconds or tapped each
foot six times on the popcorn-covered floor had nothing to
do with the Celtics' ability to beat the Knicks in overtime, I
convinced myself that it did.

The counting rituals that had started relatively innocu-
ously in childhood and brewed to completion in the Garden
became worse over time in certain ways than the physical
tics, which I was better able to control. I seemed to have no
control whatsoever over the way my mind worked—or
didn't work, it seemed to me, although I kept this theory to
myself. At Concord, I established a circle of friends with
whom I ate lunch and spent free blocks and went to the
movies the school showed on Friday nights, but the only
friend with whom I spent much time outside of school was
Caroline. She accepted my unexplained silences and puz-
zling bursts of manic energy in a nonjudgmental way that
nobody else so close to me had, before or since; sometimes it
occurred to me that if most of the time she didn't notice
anything out of the ordinary I must be doing a really good
job of putting up a normal front. Caroline and I grew up in
the same town, and she was a childhood friend of Alison's
from Nashoba, where they had been in the same class, a year
behind me. We became friends so quickly and so effortlessly
that after a few weeks it seemed we'd always known each
other, a sensation previously alien to me; I'd never met

anyone with whom I'd had such an immediate, unmistakable rapport or felt so comfortable around to relax my defensive maneuvers. Because Concord students didn't really date—during my four years there were a handful of traditional couples, whose relationships were viewed with skepticism and even condescension—and half of the student body lived on campus, it wasn't perceived as strange that Caroline and I spent so many weekends at each other's homes, often playing board games, which I love, as I get an actual rush from controlling my own set of pieces or movement in a finite space like a game board—such as Scrabble, Stratego, and Trivial Pursuit.

Caroline, and some of my other friends, sometimes did notice my tics and occasionally commented on them, and when their comments required a response I told them my doctor said I had a "nervous tic" and that I was stressed out about an upcoming test or paper, which was why it was bad at the time. When I got my license, I drove Caroline to and from school most days, and the combination of proximity and lack of distraction made her especially observant— "What are you doing!" she shrieked, on more than one occasion, as I veered precariously close to one side of the road or the other due to a tic or sat frozen through an entire green light, not hearing her voice. On the way home from a weekend on Cape Cod one summer I drove us right into the exit mouth of a one-way tunnel in Boston, unaware that I'd made a mistake—in the instant it took me to finish a tic—until the drivers in the cars headed toward us started leaning on their horns as we drove into oncoming traffic. Usually, though, comments came in the form of observations that assumed an explicable motive. You must have hurt your neck was by far the most common; You look like you could use a backrub, a close second. Most of the time, during the hours of the school day, and throughout sports practice—where physical release worked its customary magic—I managed to duck into a bathroom when I felt an unsuppressable ticcing session coming on or after having held one back for too long. Sometimes when I knew I was ticcing badly, or conspicuously, I anticipated questions or comments and rued out loud whatever future event was causing me so much discomfort that my "annoying little nervous tic" had kicked in; most of the time, but not always, that nipped comments in the bud.

One afternoon in chemistry, my least favorite subject, as it required copious note-taking, constant attention in class, and a steady workload at home, with which I was always behind, I was suddenly sure I'd been caught. In the back of the classroom, where I liked to sit so only those on either side could sense any unusual movement, I usually escaped detection. When I was late—because I'd been counting steps or trying to find the right textbook—I was forced to sit up front in the hot zone, where the whole class had a clear view of my sides and my back, making me twitchier than I liked to be in school under the best of circumstances. These were not the best of circumstances, and my seat was front-row center; many of the other kids in the class were older than I, and one of them, Katy, a notoriously sharp-tongued snotty senior, had already asked me several times over the semester about my head twitch in a bemused, slightly menacing voice.

We moved from the desks to the lab after a short lecture, and for a moment I thought I'd been handed a lucky break, until the teacher asked each pair of lab partners to team up with another pair, dividing the class into groups of four. Katy and her partner happened to be standing at the workstation next to me and my lab partner, and Katy rolled her eyes when she realized she was going to have to work with us. For a few minutes we proceeded in silence, setting up our experiment on the counter space. Then, deliberately, Katy knocked a small beaker on the floor with her elbow. Miraculously, it landed on a notebook and didn't break. "Pick it up," Katy commanded, and my lab partner and I both moved to retrieve it, but Katy stopped him with a hand on his arm, and I knelt down, taking the opportunity—these were the moments that generally saved me—to crack my neck and tap my shoe six times on a white tile in the checkerboard floor, somehow hoping this would prevent Katy from continuing to pick on me, which I knew she was set upon doing. When I stood up and placed the beaker on the lab counter, Katy's lab partner giggled nervously. Katy's head was cocked at an unlikely angle, in what was an obvious if exaggerated imitation of my neck tic. I looked at my lab partner, who avoided my eyes and began writing furiously in his lab book. After a few jerks, in the attempted manner of my twitch, Katy assumed her normal haughty posture with a self-satisfied smile.

With faltering hands, I forced myself to participate in the experiment, studiously avoiding direct interaction with Katy and holding my eyes wide open in an effort to keep them from tearing up. But as soon as the bell rang, signifying the end of the class, I grabbed my books and my bag and ran to the bathroom, where I locked myself into a stall and remained, reading a novel, for the rest of the day, skipping my afternoon classes and mumbling "Out in a second," whenever anyone banged on the door. I contemplated dropping the class, sure that further exposure to Katy would lead to an utter collapse, but quitting would have meant repeating it the following year, which was unthinkable; as it was, it would take all of my powers of memorization to pass once. For the rest of the semester I cut whatever class I had before chemistry instead, whenever I could, arriving ten minutes early so I could make myself invisible in the far rear corner of the room before the rest of the students showed up.

six ▬▬▬▬▬▬▬▬▬▬▬▬▬▬▬▬▬▬▬▬▬▬▬▬▬▬▬▬

SEISMIC SHIFTS

"**W**hat are you doing?"

I didn't hear the question at first—it was asked of me so frequently I often tuned it out unconsciously—and kept arranging my French fries.

"Earth to Amy. Is anybody in there?" Nicole rapped me on the head with characteristic zeal. I was engaged in my customary predinner ritual: If I sorted the fries into pairs before digging in, eliminating an odd man out (if there happened to be one) by placing it on the tray beneath my plate, I could proceed with abandon. Otherwise, I had to count as I ate, which required a steady flow of concentration and made it difficult to participate even superficially in conversation for much of the meal. Over the previous few years, many of my rituals had converged around food; thanks to my father I associated meals with being watched and therefore tense, and I always tried to keep especially still while sitting at a table over food. As always, when I was holding back from twitching, the impulse found an alternate outlet, in this case emerging as an obsession over what and how I ate.

Vassar's dining hall was vast and outdated in 1988, when I arrived as a freshman, with the institutional-style decor favored in the 1970s; only the presence of hundreds of students kept it from resembling a hospital cafeteria. Sometimes, when getting through a meal entailed outlasting three waves of fellow diners—as I both pretended and convinced myself I was having such a pleasant time I simply couldn't leave—it became a prison, from which I was granted only occasional parole. During my first two years of college, when I lived in the dormitories, I ate two meals a day in the dining hall, often with the same group of people, almost always including Nicole, and became quickly and intimately acquainted with the nuances of the rotating menu. Foods with too many components to count, such as cereal and noodles, could be selected only when I was feeling reckless or testing myself. Single-unit foods, such as hamburgers and hot dogs, were the safest bet, as they could be eaten in pairs of bites, totally inconspicuously. The salad bar was safest of all, a reliable fallback in spite of my dislike of most vegetables; it was entirely self-serve, affording total control over numbers and placement, although counting out chickpeas is equally tiresome and time-consuming. It didn't take too long before my new friends began to comment on my odd eating style—how I always chose similar foods, took forever to finish them, and chewed so methodically—but many college students have odd eating styles, and unlike some of the women we knew, at least I ate. I didn't mind so much having my eating habits scrutinized, anyway—it detracted from my other, less explicable bizarre behaviors, made manifest in daily dormitory life, and allowed me to assume my protective mantle of harmless, even engaging eccentricity.

Besides my extensive collections of books, clothes, records, photographs, and junk, I hoarded food in my one-room triple, well beyond the soda and beer we stored under our beds like college students everywhere. At first, my roommates were indulgent, describing me fondly as a "packrat" and humoring me as my stuff encroached on their designated areas of the room. I convinced Pam, a recycling fanatic, that it was a good idea to steal butter packets from the dining hall for our popcorn—instead of buying large and therefore wasteful pound-size boxes at the local grocery store—and store them on our window ledge. This led to other pilfered foods kept outdoors for "chilling purposes," until the morning I awoke to the startling sight of a squirrel on the inside of the ledge, lapping butter from the pat he held in his little curled paws. As I watched, spellbound and blurry-eyed in the hazy predawn light, he dropped the butter, scurried boldly across the room, and came to a stop squarely on top of a soundly sleeping Pam. Finally I screamed, and the terrified squirrel raced around the room in a panic, while Pam, Christie, and I stood on our beds shrieking, waking up our neighbors on both sides and across the hall, until the squirrel finally escaped, gratefully, through the very window he'd come in.

Later that same week, after I'd transferred my food supply to the back right corner of my enormous closet, Nicole dropped in from down the hall to hang out. I offered to prepare a snack—cheese and crackers—and dug through the piles of clothes on my floor until I could get at the large laundry basket in my closet that I'd turned into a pantry. Without detection, I'd accumulated enough sustenance to keep the entire fourth floor well fed if we happened to be snowbound in the dorm until the millennium.

"Hang on a second," I said, setting aside bags of potato chips and soda cans, in search of the crackers I knew were in there somewhere. Nicole was flipping through the CDs stacked by Pam's stereo, and she jumped to her feet when I screamed. The hair on my arms stood straight up; although I have never been afraid of mice, the unexpected light scratch of tiny claws on the back of my hand sent a shiver up my spine. A gregarious tan-and-white mouse, whom I immediately named Danny Ainge after a Boston Celtic with similar coloring, had taken up residence on my "food shelf." I kept Danny as a secret pet for a few weeks, until word leaked out to Pam and Christie, who were unfathomably tolerant of most of my habits, and willingly loaned me life's necessities, such as pencils and shampoo, when I found myself lacking them, but drew the line at resident rodents.

The hoarding was exacerbated by the care packages I received almost weekly from my father, and I'm still not sure for whom the transition from home to college was more difficult, me or him. My father's adherence to routine and dependence on continuity equals if not surpasses my own; easing his separation anxiety with a ritual, a setup I understood innately, my father had declared the previous summer that he would send me something—even if it was just a postcard—every single day for the four years I lived at Vassar, a "tradition," he maintained without fail and continued with Alison, who left for the Rhode Island School of Design the year after I'd deserted him, or been deserted, depending on whose perspective you chose. In an unintended irony, receiving the mail became one of my own strict rituals, well nourished by the steady onslaught of letters, news clippings, and packages (although often, tellingly, the day's outlay would be an index card on which the words "Nothing new here" were scrawled, sometimes abbreviated to the even less necessary "N- n- h-"). Sometimes I checked my mail twenty times a day, sometimes more. Although I knew there was precisely zero chance of a fluke delivery, I checked on Sundays too, surreptitiously, because it seemed imbalanced and therefore intolerable to skip just that one day. Today, when I am tired or under pressure, I revert to this obsession with the mail, planting myself on the stoop outside my apartment for hours at a time, waiting for the mailman to appear, forcing myself to remain seated while he sorts.

Of course I forced myself to go out, it was "normal" to do so, abnormal to feel comfortable only in the confines of a shoebox-size dorm room, and Pam was a natural extrovert who simply ignored what she perceived as my laziness-based stay-at-home tendencies. On my first night at Vassar, in fact, she dragged me to an all-campus party at the town houses, a compound where most upperclassmen live and where I was to move for my junior and senior years; I marveled that she'd even heard about it—I'd never had that knack for picking up on what was going on around me beyond the world I could see and touch. As I'd discovered and fine-tuned during high school, the artful consumption of alcohol was capable of lessening my tics, sanding off their rough edges, rendering them softer and smoother and more like acceptable stretching motions than loony, jerky ones; when a guy handed me a plastic cup full of beer I downed it immediately, thwarting the initial tics that would be sure to feed off themselves, turning toward Pam with a smile, ready to make myself socialize. As in high school, I studiously avoided cigarettes, mostly because I'd watched my aunt Ruth shrivel and die from lung cancer while I studied the disease independently and noted her slipping from stage into degenerative stage, but I didn't equate marijuana with either physical or emotional distress.

I'd tried smoking pot in high school a few times, but because I had never smoked cigarettes, I hadn't been able to get my head around the concept of inhaling and ended up just faking and exhaling the smoke I'd dutifully held in my mouth after a few seconds with a phony, stoned smile, gleaned from *Fast Times at Ridgemont High* and *The Breakfast Club*. In college, smoking pot seemed as much a part of the fabric of daily life as eating lunch or taking exams, and I had long seen the appeal of a substance capable of making me— the most physically and mentally rigid person I knew besides my father—lie limp as a dishrag even on a cement staircase, as did some of my friends who'd had more experience with the drug. One night my friend Jeanie and I were at a party she'd dragged me along to, and a mutual acquaintance asked if we wanted to get high. We followed him out to a patch of trees behind the dorm hosting the event, and he pulled a small plastic contraption out of his jacket pocket. It was a bong, the first one I'd ever seen, and it proved to be much easier to master than the joints I'd been handed in the past. The problem was, although he and Jeanie were soon lying back on the grass staring up at the patches of black, starless sky visible through the pine boughs, I didn't feel the way I thought I was supposed to. After a while I sat down next to Jeanie, whose eyes were half closed. "Jeanie," I whispered. Our supplier was now sound asleep, judging from his low, even snores.

"Yeah?" she whispered back, adding "This is great, huh? The grass is so soft." I lay down next to her. The sky looked like it always did at Vassar, clean and pure and ink-washed, as if Manhattan and all its pollution and smog were days and not hours away. I wasn't twitching, which was nice for a change, but the grass felt cold and scratchy to me, even slightly damp. The ground beneath it was hard, and although it was still early fall, I shivered and folded my arms tight across my chest for warmth.

"Aren't you cold?" I asked, but what I really wanted to know was: Why wasn't the pot working for me? Why, in fact, couldn't I ever manage to get out of myself, away from myself, for even a minute or two, especially when under the influence of a drug that turned everyone else I knew into a walking zombie?

"Nope." She sighed, and I knew she was telling the truth. "Just perfect." Her eyes fluttered shut, and I stood up, wiped pine needles off my clothes, and announced to the darkness that I was going home.

As I walked alone along the path back to my dorm, I realized that I *did* feel different, albeit in a somehow familiar way: clear-headed, maybe. It struck me that for the past half hour or so I hadn't been thinking about my body at all, not how my clothes were chafing my skin or how my joints ached from incessant flexing or how tendrils of disobedient hair were brushing against my face in the manner of a thousand cell-sized spiders. I hadn't been hyperaware of my surroundings either, not ordering them, organizing them, or connecting to them; in fact, although I usually had to lie down outdoors (and sometimes indoors as well) so as much of me as possible would be against a solid surface, I'd been standing, unsupported, for most of the time Jeanie had been prone and gazing, entranced, at the sky. With recognition, then, I named my state in a whisper; for the first time in a decade I felt unburdened, unfettered: "normal." Any passersby, had they crossed my path, would have agreed: For once I was just a person walking through the woods on a clear fall night, a college student headed back to her dorm, a regular girl in faded jeans and a suede jacket who moved through space with loose limbs and an uncluttered mind. The pot, I knew, had rendered me *me* again, but it was a version of me I only faintly recognized now; unlike alcohol, which made me drunk and loopy like anyone else as it forcefully edged me away, pot had lifted the fog, bringing me back, serving as an escape of a better, though far more frightening nature.

Later that night I lay in my bed, which *was* soft and warm, and looked up at the glow-in-the-dark stars I'd stuck to my ceiling in the shape of various, easy-to-form constellations. Most of the time they didn't glow, as only hours of exposure to bright light brought out the color. I had inadvertently left our lamps on all afternoon, though, and for once they stood out against the chipped and grimy ceiling. From that night onward, I never smoked pot unless I had also had a drink or two first; I wasn't ready to acknowledge what had become apparent to me that night under the fake constellations of my own design: If it took drugs to restore me to the self I had once been, before my tics and rituals, what did that say about the self I was now?

This presented a formidable conundrum, which plagued

me on sleepless nights for years: What was me, and what wasn't me, and what lay in between? Before I started taking medication for my disorders, before I even knew that I had a disorder at all, I considered my tics and rituals to be wholly distinct from my essential self. I lied to myself easily and often, taking immense if superficial comfort in the predominant lie: that these inexplicable movements and behaviors were somehow detachable from the real me, like a heavy backpack full of bricks and stones I was forced to carry around most of the time but could take off whenever I really wanted to. The fact that drinking or getting stoned appeared to remove the backpack for me, when I knew full well I wasn't capable of doing so in an unaltered state, made me question my most fundamental beliefs about my personality; if all of my defining traits were so flimsy as to disappear when dosed with a couple of beers, then were they really defining traits in the first place?

I tried to explain to Nicole how being—or rather not really being—stoned had changed my perception of myself, but the subject of my dual selves was largely uncharted territory in spite of her periodic minor inquisitions about my rituals and tics, and I didn't have the language or the comfort level to make her understand. "Sounds like it worked all right to me," she laughed, after my fumbled attempts to delineate the subtle but essential shift, and I mumbled "I guess so," wanting to believe. Like Caroline, who was still at Concord Academy, finishing her senior year, Nicole didn't seem to live in two worlds—constantly engaged in patrolling the border—and assumed the way I was with her was simply the way I was all the time. As had been true with Caroline too, I found myself coveting her very effortlessness, the apparent absence of shadowy cor-

ners and Pandora's boxes nailed firmly shut behind impenetrable walls. I kept close, watched carefully, hoping her natural
ease would somehow rub off on me; I didn't mind existing
outside the epicenter of campus life, but my status in my own
little world was everything, perhaps because I had so much
trouble establishing connections beyond it. Sometimes I felt
my foothold on my persona grow shaky, wondered if I had
crossed over into distastefully weird from charmingly odd,
grew convinced that my friends and dormmates discussed my
twitching in hushed, disgusted voices when I wasn't around,
although I never caught anyone in the act.

Maintaining my charade was taking its toll, mostly in the
amount of time I spent in virtual hiding, and I made a rule
that I would leave my room once a day other than for meals
or class in order to expand my increasingly narrow horizons.
Soon, through Nicole, I met Ben, a childhood friend of hers
from San Francisco who'd also ended up at Vassar, and Greg
and Mish, Ben's inseparable companions. As always, I reveled
in hanging out with what I'd decided was the generally less
observant and therefore less critical gender—although this
theory had one gaping hole in the emphatic form of my father, whose powers of observation and capacity for making
me self-conscious far outshone those of all the women I
knew. Shooting pool, throwing darts, driving to the area's
only mall in Ben's decrepit car became preferable even to
holing up in my nest, as the constant physical activity and
high energy level I found in the orbit Ben and his friends in-
habited kept me relatively twitch-free, and away from my
room I could forget about its constantly multiplying contents and their careful arrangements.

I attended classes selectively, based on factors and rules

that made sense only to me; lectures, held in large, dim rooms, were my preference, as it was easy to appear invisible among so many faces. Seminars were bad, and discussion groups led by professors who called on students randomly were anathemas, as unanticipated questions sent me into conspicuous spasms, not to mention that the smaller the class, the more likely the professor was to notice and single me out, by virtue of the fact that I was often the only person in the room who was moving. Just as security guards always take me for a potential shoplifter because I compulsively touch clothes and twitch while browsing, which they interpret as furtive expressions of guilt, professors always thought I was raising my hand when I wasn't. Tourette's has made me an expert on the misinterpreted gesture, has had the unexpected benefit of teaching me to watch faces for unintentional crinkles, to listen for an unavoidable change in pitch or tone. On the flip side, like a congenitally deaf person who has never mastered the nuances of vocal speech, I am not particularly deft at throwing out signals of my own.

One evening in our sophomore spring Ben and I were playing Mac Yahtzee on my computer in my tiny room when he suddenly kissed me. We'd been spending a lot of time alone together, as Nicole and Greg had both acquired significant others and were flush in the throes of couple-dom, but nothing Ben had said or done up to this point had prepared me for this; in fact, I'd marveled to Caroline over the phone that I was capable of having such a close male friend without having to confront the issue of sex. Over the preceding year we had been alone in a variety of situations, in the car on the way to the Galleria, Poughkeepsie's primary commercial offering, at meals, shooting pool in the basement of his dorm. I didn't twitch much around him anymore, when it was just the two of us, and the thought of upsetting that balance caused my eyes to roll up in my head. With the exception of Tim—and we know how that ended—I made the first move with men, allowing me to maneuver a situation to my advantage and maintain control as much as possible; my immediate response to Ben's kiss was to pull away and fold my arms tight to avert the uncontrollable tics such an event was sure to provoke. A few nights later, though, in one of the few impromptu acts of my life, I led him back to my room after a party we'd left early in unspoken concordance, and we started a relationship of sorts, which lasted off and on for the rest of our time at Vassar. Although for a long while I didn't tell a soul about our periodic rendezvous, the still grayness of the dew-soaked quad just before dawn, what it was like to wake up in the middle of the night with another body clutching the sheets and making them fall unevenly across the bed (I liked them perpendicular to my body, and I slept precisely in the center of my bed), thinking about Ben and trying to decide how I could emerge from the entanglement unscathed—so I could return to my safe and solitary existence—occupied many waking hours.

One of the reasons, I think, I was able to enter into this relationship, albeit a largely secret one, when I had avoided intimacy of all kinds for years, was the fact that Ben never commented on my tics, not even when we'd spent enough time alone together that there was no chance he hadn't noticed them. The more intimate our relationship grew, the more I ticced in his presence, unsure how to navigate these foreign, turbulent waters, but he still never said a word. After

one episode in his bedroom when I'd fallen prey to a con-
torted and complicated full-body twitch lasting at least a full
minute (one friend always announces, "She's stuck again!"
when it happens today) he didn't so much as raise an eye-
brow, kept folding his laundry as if nothing had happened.

"Did you *see* that?" I finally asked, wondering if it was
possible he was storing up his mockery for later, to share
with Greg and his other friends; maybe my normal act was
losing its panache. The twitch had left me drained and knot-
ted, and without a word, Ben came up behind me and
started rubbing my shoulders, easing the ache.

"What, your tic?" He sounded surprised by the question.

"Yes, my tic," I blurted, turning to face him and shaking
off his hands, wondering how and where he'd picked up the
term. "I just jerked around in front of you like a crazy person, and you stood there not saying a word."

"What do you want me to say?" he said. I was stumped. I
certainly didn't want him to tell me to leave immediately,
that I was a freakish object of contempt no longer desirable
as a friend or anything else. But then again, confirmation
that he didn't perceive me as crazy, that my body sometimes
acted on its own and that he knew that, would maybe have
lifted an as-yet-unacknowledged burden.

"Do you hate it when I twitch?" I asked, changing tactics. "Does it embarrass you?"

"To tell you the truth," he answered, "I barely even notice it anymore." I rode on that for the rest of the year.

When Ben announced shortly before graduation that he
was moving to Boston (where I was headed) in spite of my
protests and had found an affordable, two-bedroom apart-

ment just outside Harvard Square thanks to a friend of his uncle's, I felt trapped. Although I knew that Ben, as usual, found my denial of our relationship (which had increased in intensity over our junior and senior years) annoying and a semantic splitting of hairs, he was stubborn and unwilling to give up on me yet. He knew that having my own room— even if we both slept in it at night—would be the deciding factor in my acceptance and played this up as a selling point. It went unsaid, but he also knew the prospect of my under-going an apartment search alone—with all the unpre-dictable encounters and responsibilities such an undertaking entails—was less likely even than acquiescence. He was right on both counts; the thought of returning to crowded arrangements such as I'd endured in college, sharing living space and snatching moments alone for optimal twitching, was profoundly distasteful. If any fact had emerged from my college experience it was that the only way I could get out of bed in the morning and make it through the rest of the day with any semblance of normalcy was to maintain utter control over my surroundings. After an hour spent scanning the incomprehensible rental listings, I agreed to a test-run.

Once I had found permanent homes in our new apart-ment for my belongings—my childhood comforter, favorite books, special shells, coins, photographs, and countless other talismans, I preserved the arrangements with a curator's eye, removing Ben's socks, newspapers, and pens many times each day from what was essentially a museum. My bedroom, more than any other place, has always been the safe house of my tics and rituals, the one environment in which I am ever free to move and manipulate as I see fit. It is where I keep my clothes, in an alphabetical system established long ago;

shared closet space would have been an unequivocal deal-breaker, but the apartment had plenty of closets. Dresser drawers had a system all their own, equally unsuited for co-existence. Desk space was virtually sacred, as my desk is where I write. Ben claimed to understand, and at first significant conflicts were few and far between, although I insisted on a daily basis to him, my parents, and all of my friends that we were not "living together" but merely capitalizing on a convenient and practical setup.

Obsessive-compulsive disorder is clever, ironically so; like many OCD sufferers, although I have a deserved reputation as a slob, my oppressive sense of order is its formidable peer. I cannot work if my surroundings don't feel right; as I sit at my computer I can point out dozens of microcosmic systems within the span of my arms that enable me to keep typing, to write one word and then the next, without getting up to perform one of a thousand rituals that remain dormant and pop out on the most inopportune occasions, such as an impending deadline. Now, for example, the objects on my desk are arranged in an arc around my computer. The phone is to the left, on top of its instruction manual. This is because I have not yet read the manual; the phone is new. All over my apartment instruction manuals for various appliances and electronic equipment can be found evenly placed beneath the objects they demystify. Next to the phone is the digital alarm clock I have had for fifteen years; if you look closely you can see the remains of a chocolate bar I left on the top in high school melted into the lines that constitute the speaker; I grow as attached to objects as I do to people—maybe more so—and a fear of being disloyal keeps me well stocked with countless useless possessions.

The alarm is set for 7:30; for as long as I can remember I have never set a clock for a time that did not end on an even number, a "habit" I recently learned I share with my father. Like him, I do not get out of bed in the morning until the minute digit is even. In fact, I operate on an even minute system for all things: leaving the apartment, making important phone calls, programming the microwave and the VCR. To the right of the clock is my pen and pencil cup. I cannot tolerate loose pens and pencils; several times a day I will circulate the apartment on a mission to retrieve and confine any that have managed to escape recklessly from their home by, say, being used. My mouse pad is to the right of my computer, parallel to it, and a stack of papers I have collected for a magazine article I hope to write is to the right of the mouse pad, also parallel.

Early on in what I thought of as our living experiment, I met a friend for dinner one night and returned to find that Ben had decided to work in my room for a "change of pace." He was immediately banished, as I set to work righting the various wrongs; later he said, with a rare lack of sensitivity and flash of indignance, "Sometimes I think you really are nuts." Nuts, I thought to myself, still retrieving pens from under the bed and straightening manuals left askew, was being so intrusive as to invade my private space in my absence. Nuts, I decided, was thinking this arrangement was ever going to work in the first place. The only place I would be able to live a normal life was on a deserted island.

Living in such close proximity with another person, even someone who knew me as well and loved me as much as Ben, was proving more difficult than I'd imagined, in ways I'd never anticipated. No longer were third parties lurking in the wings on whom I could deflect any rituals or rules I'd established; every off-kilter, controlling move I made was attributed immediately and resentfully to me. Sometimes I was unsure if my demands were unreasonable but sane, or truly beyond my control. When Ben brought home a new couch for the living room as a surprise, I stomped up to my room and slammed the door.

"What's wrong?" he said, through the door, where he could hear me throwing a tennis ball against the wall, which I did when I was too angry to speak. "If you don't like it, we don't have to keep it." Squeezing the ball, I threw open the door.

"How could you make such a decision without me?" I yelled. "Do you have any idea how I feel about placement?"

"I know where I'd like to place you sometimes," he muttered, jogging down the stairs, followed by the tennis ball, which I hurled at his retreating head.

Without the distractions of family or dorm life, my compulsiveness pushed its way to the forefront and became my defining and guiding characteristic. Certain "habits" became sore spots, never given time to heal; each passing day exacerbated the wounds of misunderstanding. When Ben discovered soured milk or moldy cheese in the refrigerator, he reacted with disgust, not tolerance. And although I didn't know why I held on to spoiled food—it was never financially necessary for me to use turned dairy products in baked goods or cut green rinds off shriveled hunks of cheddar for frittata after frittata (a dish that could incorporate pretty much any leftovers)—I resented having to hide things from him in my own home. When he tried to change the radio station I played twenty-four hours a day, or set the alarm for

6:15 instead of the infinitely preferable 6:16, I couldn't rationalize my discomfort, so I expressed my inflexibility as anger, then—later—rage.

The regular routine I established—wake up, go to work, come home, read in bed—was as unforgiving as a steel trap. If Ben wanted to take a different path as we walked to the subway in the morning, and I complied (more often than not I just told him I'd see him at the station, pretending I had to stop in at a certain store or the post office on the way), I'd feel ill at ease for the rest of the day. If at work, where I guarded my tiny office with the protective instincts of a mother lion, a coworker moved my files or inadvertently rearranged my office supplies, I could not resume editing or filing until I'd restored order to the chaos; a borrowed message pad once set me on a search mission that could not have been undertaken more seriously if I'd lost a priceless family heirloom. Due more to my own skyrocketing fears than anything Ben said or did, I became paranoid, convinced that my tics, and not my more obvious control issues, were driving us apart, and the paranoia made the tics even worse.

"You can't look at me," I would shout accusingly after my tics had been particularly bad for a few days and Ben was watching TV or reading the newspaper, in what I assumed was an attempt to avoid me. "You hate it when I twitch."

"No," he'd say patiently or, later, not so patiently, "That's not true and you know it. But I do wish we could throw away the newspapers."

Starting in college, my OCD made an executive decision that no newspaper, magazine, or catalog that so much as entered my living space could be discarded without being read from cover to cover, every last word, including ads and headlines. I resisted subscribing to either the *Boston Globe* or the *New York Times,* opting instead to read certain preselected selections outside of the house, but still, the periodicals flooded the downstairs, crept up the staircase, and eventually covered most of the floor and counter space throughout our three-room apartment. One day, home sick from work, I read twenty-six magazines from cover to cover, until I fell asleep in the middle of an article on money market funds in a magazine the mailman had delivered by mistake.

For many years now, over summers and holiday vacations at home, my mother had been trying to convince me to "talk to someone" about my tics; I never verbalized what were for me the equally worrisome, taxing internal manifestations, so it didn't occur to her that they might also require professional attention. By "talk to someone" she meant see a psychologist, because she assumed, as I did, that my tics had psychological origins and were most likely related to anxiety, as my pediatrician had insinuated so long ago. Although this was never stated overtly, anxiety was my father's defining characteristic, and I'm sure it occurred to all of us at one point or another that my tics were nothing more or less than my extreme means of expressing my inherited constitution. Whenever she gently broached the subject, though, I asked her politely to drop it, and for the most part I meant it; as far as I was concerned, I had managed to live so far with the immense sum of the weird things I did to a tolerable extent, and if I could just keep other people from noticing most of the time I'd be able to live an outwardly—if not an inwardly—normal life. Occasionally I'd wonder if I was fooling myself, kneeling outside our apartment in two inches of slushy mud sifting through the trash can for the pennies Ben sometimes threw away when I wasn't around, or painstak-ingly climbing a flight of stairs stepping six times with each foot on each step, but I always managed to convince myself that willpower and determination—of which I had no shortage—would ultimately prevail.

But I knew it too; for no discernible reason, my tics had been especially bad of late, maybe worse than ever before, and thoughts of the inevitable sway toward normal I knew they'd take eventually—they always did—offered little solace. Occa-sionally I wondered if anxiety had little to do with my tics and habits themselves but plenty to do with the way refusing to confront them was making me feel, but I remained con-vinced that whatever my mother—or some psychologist—suggested, jogging or, God forbid, yoga, was not going to make me stop twitching. I twitched when I was tired, hungry, cold, excited, angry, relaxed, and, worst of all from my per-spective, as it seemed to indicate an utter lack of stimulus, alone. Pondering this, for the first time in my life I made my-self evaluate the tics and habits as an entity, a group of maybe related, definitely intrusive compulsions that had an effect on everything I did. I started composing a list-in-progress of all that could qualify as abnormal, first mentally, then on a piece of paper I carried around with me at all times, moving it from pocket to pocket, switching it from bag to bag, tucking it under my pillow at night when I slept. Ben soon noticed my new obsession, which must have struck him as comparatively harmless but certainly indicative of something.

"What's that?" he asked, when he caught me scribbling away in the middle of the night. "What are you doing?"

"I'm not sure yet," I said, not looking up from my list. "But I think it's important."

The next day I called the physician at Brigham and Women's Hospital who'd been my primary-care doctor throughout college. She was out to lunch, and a receptionist asked if I wanted to leave a message on her voice mail. So I wouldn't lose my resolve I said yes, but when the beep went off, I had nothing to say. I had never tried, even to myself, to put into words the whole of what I knew instinctively was wrong with me, had known for years. "You are not insane," I said to myself, for strength, relishing the unplanned quartet, and then I was able to speak. "Dr. Liebner," I said, "it's been a couple of years and you might not remember me, but this is Amy Wilensky and I think I have OCD."

I'm not sure where I'd even picked up the term; in the early 1990s, it was not yet part of the vernacular, but its occasional presence in the media had obviously left an impression. Later that afternoon the phone rang, and I jumped, so physically agitated I wasn't sure I was going to reach it in time. Struggling to keep still, I grasped the handset and heard Dr. Liebner's puzzled voice; it took us a few minutes to establish that I had not been merely providing her with an update on my current state of mind but attempting, awkwardly, to request a referral. In a voice that revealed no surprise, she gave me a couple of names, recommended one guy in particular, a psychologist with a private practice in Brookline, and I wrote down his number on a scrap of paper ripped from the phone book. After she'd wished me luck and signed off, I tucked the scrap into my wallet, as opposed to the depths of my bag or the back pocket of a pair of cords I wouldn't wear again for six months, where such scraps usually wound up, regardless of urgency. Once in a while, on the subway or seeking safe haven in a ladies' room, I'd remove the dingy scrap and open it, but I always refolded it on the creases and placed it back inside; it was enough for awhile to know it was there.

That fall I applied to graduate schools for creative writing. Without telling anyone, including Ben, I sent an application to Columbia, although I'd always sworn I could never live outside of greater Boston. My brief conversation with Dr. Liebner had created a slight but certain shift in my deeply ingrained rigidity. Change, my lifelong enemy, beckoned enticingly, and for once its siren call held a note of appeal. When the Columbia acceptance letter arrived in the mail, instead of filing it wistfully, I kept it out on my desk, aligning its corners with affection, reading and rereading it, imagining myself living in New York. Caroline had gone to Columbia as an undergraduate and stayed there; that was a plus—when I wasn't writing I could stake out a spot for myself on her new floor and rediscover the games that drew me in so beguilingly, kept me twitch-free and at ease. My publishing job was increasingly unbearable—I spent up to a quarter of each day at the office in the ladies' room—and there could no longer be any doubt I was unsuited to domesticity. If either Ben or I didn't leave our apartment soon, it would house two crazy people instead of just one.

Ben agreed that Columbia was an opportunity too good to pass up. Like me, or so he said, he thought we'd get along better if we saw each other only on weekends and over vacations for a while, and we both pretended that once I started classes, and throughout my two years of school in Manhattan, our relationship would remain intact. I knew Ben was pretty sure we'd get married someday. Occasionally he veered into forbidden territory, talking about the future, discussing children's names and drawing plans for the farm he wanted us to buy and restore in Vermont. Such assumptions made me back off as though facing attack; irrevocable decisions of any kind were well beyond my ken. My imminent departure became my primary concern, and in an unexpected, alarming twist, it was making me reckless.

"HEY, LADY! Are you crazy?" The kid who pulled me from the edge of the subway platform in downtown Boston was about twenty, not so much younger than me. Sometimes when "nothing feels right," making things even less right— teetering on a precipice—is the only option. I mumbled something inarticulate, hoping he'd assume I'd thanked him, and made my way to a bench before he could persist or attract unwanted attention. Forcing myself to sit down, I removed the Columbia course catalog from my bag. I could feel the kid's eyes still on me; it was midafternoon and the station was deserted. Finally the proverbial light at the end of the tunnel appeared, and the train, which had been just a rumble in the distance when he'd yanked me away, pulled up and screeched to a stop. I made sure we got on different cars.

Since I'd started thinking in concrete terms about moving to New York, I'd been fighting a daily powerful urge to jump off the subway platform onto the tracks. I didn't *want* to jump down, I had no desire to either injure myself or terrify onlookers, but I felt, and still feel sometimes, the need to get down there on the tracks, where I'm not supposed to be. The methods were different each time; when I'd been "rescued" by the boy I'd decided I had to stand on the absolute edge of the platform with each foot exactly halfway over, a stance requiring precarious balance, or the gesture "would not count." The risk-taking fed off itself, severed me from my powers of judgment and reason; I was suddenly a slave to the urges, instead of their wimpy master. Narrowly, I missed being hit by hundreds of cars as I walked headlong into busy streets to step on manhole covers. At home, I banged my head against my bedroom wall, not ever hard enough to knock myself out, but coming very, very close. Driving, I closed my eyes when approaching intersections, pinned my chin to my chest when turning left, pressed the gas pedal all the way to the floor on the highway. At a friend's apartment I sat one evening before dawn on the rooftop deck grasping the rails with both hands, counting, to erase the thought from my head that I was about to jump thirty-two stories to the ground. Other than stupidity, the only quality these compulsions shared was a built-in defense mechanism that prevented me from following through.

This was the summer I knew. Performing dangerous, irrational, even life-threatening stunts with no will to do so convinced me, finally, that I needed help, had to dial the number on the scrap in my wallet before I hurt myself or, worse, somebody else. Later I was immensely gratified to learn that self-injurious behavior is endemic to Tourette's; some sufferers have intrusive, agonizing fears they will maim or kill a loved one, although they never actually do so; others hurt themselves in small but impactful ways, as I was, more and more. The evening I found myself holding a razor blade to the thick skin of my big toe was the evening I finally knew I needed a change, knew I had to go to New York.

In the summer Little, Brown, where I worked, has

"summer hours," which means everyone goes into work a half hour early Monday through Thursday and gets to leave Friday at one. The Friday a week before Ben and Alison deposited me unceremoniously in Morningside Heights I headed home, heroically forgoing my routine of whiling away the afternoon at the colorful haymarket held on the outskirts of Boston's North End. It was humid, and the T was a sauna, but as I walked to our apartment from the Central Square stop I felt cool and unaffected, stepping squarely and confidently in the center of each block in the sidewalk. As soon as I pushed open the front door the coolness vanished: Johnson, Ben's sweet-tempered but weak-stomached dog, had thrown up again on the living room floor. We didn't have air conditioning, and the apartment was a furnace from June through September; over the course of the afternoon the vomit had half-baked into the wood. I cleaned up the mess; on previous occasions Ben had told me to leave it for him, but the stench was unbearable in the heat, and I was grateful for the chance to procrastinate. When I'd scrubbed the boards until they shone, I sat down to catch my breath. The phone loomed large, an ominous presence in the thick, still air. I fumbled in my bag for my wallet and came up empty, positive proof—as if I needed it—that it had been a bad couple of weeks.

I dumped the bag's contents on the table. The bulk of the heap was paper scraps: magazine articles I'd ripped out to save or pass on, unpaid bills, loose checks to be cashed or filled out, chewed and hardened wads of gum rolled in their wrappers, hard candies covered with lint, reminders I'd written to myself, postcards to be mailed, letters I'd opened and others still sealed in their envelopes, take-out menus and matches from restaurants all over Boston and beyond. I emptied my pants and jacket pockets too, contributing half-melted chocolate bars, pieces of branches and leaves, bits of plastic, movie-ticket stubs, pebbles, and soda can flip-tops to the assemblage. Johnson, with an expression that vaguely resembled repentance, and Rory, our inscrutable cat, sat side by side on the hideous lime-green sofa, watching. When I was completely purged of all but the clothes on my body, I opened and emptied my wallet, which had appeared, miraculously, in the middle of the giant pile. I called the shrink.

I don't know what I expected the office to look like—probably something out of a Woody Allen movie—but not the suburban house I pulled up to, so twitchy I could barely let myself out of the car, sufficiently agitated to emit the indicative high-pitched squeaks only my sister has ever heard before. Letting myself in (where was the sinister Nurse Ratchett figure in a gleaming-white lab coat?), I walked up a narrow flight of stairs to a small waiting area, featuring a floor-size Oriental rug, two worn armchairs, and the ubiquitous assortment of magazines. The magazines were of a quality a step above those in my regular doctor's and dentist's offices, I noticed; instead of *People,* the shrink had *The New Yorker,* in favor of *Women's Day, Harper's* and *The New Republic.* Briefly I found this reassuring—other crazy people liked the same magazines I did—but then I was angry. What kind of snobs were these pathetic shrink-seekers who couldn't solve their piddling problems on their own? I read *People,* secretly, and I wasn't above sneaking a peek at a *Women's Day* if my grandmother happened to have one lying around. I didn't want to be a member of this oh-so-particular club. I was almost to the door when the shrink himself appeared and gestured me in.

His office looked just like the waiting room, except bigger, and there really was a Freudian-style couch with only one arm up against the wall, a piece of furniture I would have called a chaise longue if I'd known I'd pronounce it correctly. I wasn't sure if I wanted to lie on the couch or not—it seemed more authentic to do so (and I figured if I was going to do this at all, I shouldn't do it halfway), but it also seemed more definitive, certifiable proof of the need for subsequent treatment. He saved me from having to make a defining decision by pointing at the chair facing his desk, which I took as a sign that he had high hopes for me, had deemed me on sight to be chair-worthy and therefore not entirely insane. I gripped the arms of the chair.

"So." The psychologist looked into my eyes. I felt a squeal coming on and made it a nervous giggle instead. "Tell me why you're here."

I realized the loud tapping sound echoing in my head was my own foot kicking the leg of my chair, and I planted my feet on identical patches of the kaleidoscopic rug. "Well," I stalled, "I'm here because I think I have a problem."

"And what kind of a problem is that?" he said. I felt toyed with; I'd told him over the phone I was worried about OCD, his touted area of expertise.

"Well, I have tics," I started, and then talked nonstop for the next forty minutes without once referring to the updated laundry list of symptoms I'd brought along as a safety net. I described my litany of obsessions and compulsions and showed him every tic I could remember, from the initial neck twitch on up through current renditions, including the ever-unpopular teeth click and the pinched-nerve-inducing shoulder roll. When he glanced at the clock on the wall, I stopped, waiting for him to acknowledge the torrent of information that had spilled from me so undiluted. I held my breath, counting to push the words "delusional" and "weak-willed" from my head, thinking "lack of self-control" as I tapped my feet to the rhythm of the words, adding an extra tap for the crucial sixth syllable beat.

"You have obsessive-compulsive disorder," he said, and my arms and legs relaxed; I hadn't realized how tightly I'd been clenching every available muscle and joint. "I'd be happy to take you on for therapy," he continued, as the letters OCD ran through my mind in sets of two, "and I'd also like you to try medication. There are a variety of options, but we'll have to find you a psychiatrist." I barely heard a word of this, so focused was I on the letters, crisp and finite as pairs; I could say them without really moving my mouth. "But your tics seem to indicate the presence of another disorder that often is found in conjunction with OCD. Have you ever heard of Tourette's?" This snapped me back. I stood, mumbled something about New York, and ran down the stairs. But I kept running: right past my car, through the parking lot, to a pay phone I'd noticed across the street on the drive in. I dialed my father's office number. Before he could so much as spit out "hello" I shouted into the receiver, enunciating so there'd be no need to repeat. I did not need to plan what to say; I'd been waiting for this moment for over a decade.

"I have a neurological disorder," I enunciated carefully.

"You were wrong. I was right. I can't make myself stop."
Then I hung up. I did not call this doctor back. I didn't tell
anyone, not Ben or my parents, what he'd said about
Tourette's. I drove home and screened my calls for the rest of
the day.

seven

AND THEN THERE WERE TWO

I was headed for Dodge Hall, where all of my workshops and seminars were held, to meet with my thesis advisor, Richard Locke, who also happened to be the head of the writing division and therefore perpetually overbooked. Sitting idly on the couch in the student lounge, I scanned the purple section of the previous week's *USA Today.* I made a futile stab at the *New York Times* crossword. A few people I knew wandered in and out, checking their mailboxes or their e-mail; a first-year poet was sobbing in the corner by the window, but I didn't even know her name, so I let her cry undisturbed. Finally, after about half an hour, I was alone.

My eye traveled to the front wall of the student lounge where about fifteen wire baskets were laid out on shelves; when they weren't set straight I straightened them, but this day someone had beaten me to the task. They held student work: poems, essays, stories, or chunks of novels that had been written for various classes and workshops. When it was your week in a given class you had to have your piece Xeroxed and placed in the appropriate basket in plenty of time for your classmates to pick it up and preview it for the upcoming discussion. In my first year, I'd developed a bad habit of stealing workshop pieces from the other nonfiction class baskets in order to both check out the competition and combat the boredom that set in whenever I was waiting in the student lounge. I'd never been told it was forbidden, but I had a feeling it wasn't encouraged; as is the case in many nonfiction writing classes, people tended toward the confessional: Incest, eating disorders, and wild sexual escapades were the rule rather than the exception when it came to subject matter.

I checked the basket of a workshop that I knew from previous snooping experience included a student who enjoyed writing bizarre X-rated sci-fi material that, if really nonfiction, made him much, much weirder than I. It wasn't his week. The other nonfiction workshop was mostly first-years, none of whom I knew more than slightly and none of whose work had yet acquired a reputation of any kind. The top piece was by a student named Bryant Palmer. It was called "Shakes," which gave nothing away but spoke to me nonetheless, but I hadn't even had time to scan the first page when I heard footsteps in the hallway headed in the direction of the lounge. Quickly I settled back into a corner of the couch, concealing the essay behind the now-crumpled *USA Today*.

I'd met Bryant a few weeks before at a dinner/reading I'd cohosted with my friend and fellow second-year student

Kristen in order to give the first-year nonfiction students an opportunity to meet us and talk about the program. Bryant had struck me as sweet but naive. I remembered both his thick Southern accent and Carolyn, the woman I'd erroneously assumed was his girlfriend. Bryant and Carolyn had been best friends at Vanderbilt, I learned as I read, and had never dated, and Bryant was from Alabama, of all places on earth. I'd never met anyone from Alabama before, but I guessed that accounted for the accent. I flipped to the second page. By the time I finished, I was shaking myself.

"Shakes" was about Bryant's experiences as a lifelong sufferer of Tourette's syndrome, and with few exceptions, the symptoms he described mirrored my own, down to his very recent diagnosis. Some of his "habits" and thought patterns and life experiences were virtually identical to mine, although I couldn't fathom a background—Southern, rural, religious—so different from my own. I couldn't understand how someone could know so much about me, about the parts of me I never talked about and spent every waking moment trying to suppress and ignore. When Bryant described the ways in which his father had always reacted to his tics—with an initial confusion that grew quickly into anger and shame—it was as if I'd discovered a twin from whom I'd been separated at birth; I'd never even imagined being able to explain exactly how that particular rejection felt to anyone else. When I was finally summoned in for my meeting, I would have been hard-pressed to remember my name, let alone the subject of my master's thesis, but I sat through it in a daze and sprinted home in the rain as soon as I could make my escape. Later I realized my heels were bleeding from blisters caused by the friction of my wet feet rubbing against my new boots.

Back at the apartment I shared with Caitlin, I was relieved to find myself alone. I finally located our copy of the student phone list under a stack of magazines and called Bryant Palmer. He wasn't home, so I left a message.

"Hi," I began, trying to sound friendly and sane. "You probably don't know who I am, but I read something of yours and I really have to talk to you. Please call me back as soon as you get this message." I added as an afterthought—it almost didn't seem necessary—"Oh, and this is Amy Wilensky." Then I sat down to wait. At about eight that evening Bryant returned my call, sounding guarded, as if he feared he might have unknowingly committed some first-year violation or was about to be pegged for a hazing ritual. He seemed puzzled when I told him I wanted to talk to him about his essay; I was in none of his classes and held no position of authority that would have provided me aboveground access to his work. But he agreed to see me the following day; I think he was afraid I'd show up at his apartment unannounced if he refused.

We met the next day for coffee in Dodge Hall's new coffee bar. We both arrived early, which I was soon to find out was an aberration fueled by curiosity on both of our parts.

"What did your parents say?" I asked, before we were sitting down at the rickety table. "And did you tell all your friends?" Never before had I been able to say to someone "And what about the thinking-in-balance thing?" and have them know what I meant. I'd never shared my habits and tics so openly with anyone, even the psychologist I'd talked to back in Boston. Although at the time Bryant blinked his eyes and I flexed my neck, many of our internalized habits were identical, or variations on a theme. Both of us had endured a variety of shifting tics, and many of those had overlapped over time. I asked Bryant if he had ever "talked to someone," using my mother's euphemism, and he told me that just the day before, at his own mother's suggestion, he'd met with a Columbia psychologist named Dr. Iager and found her un-expectedly sympathetic and warm. He gave me her number.

Knowing that someone as well rounded and smart and funny and highly functioning as Bryant had whatever it was that I had gave me the push I needed to face my disorders head-on. Dr. Iager confirmed that I had Tourette's and OCD—I didn't tell her about the Boston shrink—embar-rassed, I guess, that I'd let the diagnosis suffice for so long without seeking help. She explained that I had what is called a "spectrum disorder," meaning that my tics, obsessions, and compulsions did not fall into one neat category—such as blinking or checking or washing—but rather touched on many, often at once. Easing my fears that I'd been unlucky enough to be born with two unrelated neurological disor-ders, she told me that Tourette's and OCD were often part-ners in crime, that many people with Tourette's had inte-grally related OCD. My vocal tics—clicking my teeth, pressing my tongue against the roof of my mouth until it made a sucking sound, having words get stuck in my throat when I am flexing the muscles, and the rare but strangest high-pitched squeals—were part of Tourette's, as were the externally visible tics and the internally destructive habits, my excess energy, constant motion, inability to concentrate, and surely much, much more. Like the Boston doctor, she recommended a combination of behavioral therapy and medication; she suggested I read a book called *Stop Obsessing: How to Overcome Your Obsessions and Compulsions* to set me on the right track and told me she'd like to refer me to someone outside Columbia when I was ready, a specialist in Tourette's who could prescribe and then modify medication and find me a trained behavioral therapist who could take on the OCD simultaneously. I left her office feeling pounds lighter, closer to the sky, striding across the bustling campus with newfound resolve.

I AM AT HOME in bookstores and libraries as I am almost nowhere else. Rooms full of books have a smell all their own and a liberating constancy, with shelves walls of words in every direction. Books require no interaction, unions of bodies or thoughts; in fact, connections with others are largely discouraged in book worlds, as most people prefer solitude for browsing and choosing. I asked a sales clerk at the Columbia bookstore where I could find the psychology section and forced myself not to look to either side as I walked there, knowing one glimpse of a sought-after novel or cookbook would break my concentration, thwart my mission for sure.

I am not a person who tends to have visceral reactions. I rarely cry, throw up, scream, or clutch at others while watching horror movies. I almost never lose my appetite or overeat when I'm upset; I do not flinch when faced with violence or gore. But as I stood in that bookstore that afternoon, one of dozens of students with a loaded backpack and a grungy baseball cap worn brim-side back, and tried to make myself look inconspicuously sane, I actually shivered with sheer anticipation. The first book that caught my eye seemed somehow familiar; later I learned it was the classic in the field of OCD: Judith Rapoport's *The Boy Who Couldn't Stop Washing*. Rapoport, a therapist with years of experience studying and treating sufferers of OCD, discussed what I had previously imagined were my own—and maybe Bryant's too—bizarre and private rituals with sufficient detachment to let me keep reading, prevent me from pushing the information away by counting the letters on the page or rereading every sixth word six times before moving on. After I'd scanned a couple of chapters just standing there, I plucked the only two other books that seemed relevant—Dr. Iager's suggestion, and one called *Living with Tourette Syndrome*, by a woman named Elaine Fantle Shimberg—and paid for them in exact change without establishing eye contact with the sales clerk; maybe, I thought, she'd take me for an extraordinarily disheveled and nervous psychiatry resident.

At three o'clock that morning I finally shut off my bedroom light, the books devoured, so wired I knew it would take me even longer to fall asleep than usual. *Stop Obsessing* featured a questionnaire with thirty-seven statements to be checked when they applied, statements such as "I avoid touching certain things because of possible contamination," in categories called Washing and Cleaning, Checking and Repeating, Ordering, Hoarding, Thinking Rituals, and Worries and Pure Obsessions. I checked all but four items. *Living with Tourette Syndrome* opened with the author's observations of her own child. Shimberg writes, "One day we simply became aware that our seven-year-old little girl was doing 'it' again. 'It' was just a shrug of her shoulders. Nothing more.

But wait . . . soon it became a shrug combined with a neck jerk, as though she had a crick in her neck. And it seemed to happen not once, but constantly. She began to complain that her neck ached."

In the space of a week I had received validation, not just from Bryant and a mental health professional, but from the dozens of people described in the pages of these books. I was surprised to learn that not everyone with OCD had one easily summed-up obsession and subsequent compulsive behavior, like hand-washing or checking the stove; most sufferers seemed to have what's called a "spectrum disorder," like mine, encompassing hundreds of obsessions and compulsions and not so easy to categorize. Learning that Tourette's was not a death sentence or a recipe for lifelong isolation came as a tremendous relief, and better still, almost all of the information in the books pointed in the direction of treatment: not a cure, exactly, that didn't seem to exist, but a management style that sounded a whole lot better than what I'd taken for granted would always be the way I lived my life.

In the following days I resumed my previous summer's list of tics and habits. Behaviors I'd never thought to analyze suddenly made sense, got factored in. Sometimes when Rory is sprawled on the floor, in that way cats have that makes them look like they're actually part of the floorboards—inexplicable, furry protuberances that just happen to have sprung up in the living room—I will join her. This started when I was in second grade and we got our first two cats, Midnight and her sister Misty. I didn't start lying with them on the floor to keep from twitching, however, although that was certainly a pleasant side effect. Rather, I noticed how the cats kept warm on certain patches of floor conveniently located in front of the heating vents. My parents, both born and bred in New England, inherited the region's gene for a very specialized kind of cheapness that prohibits heating freezing homes with anything but good old-fashioned fire. When winter had come and gone, though, and the house was then too hot (the gene extends to an avoidance of air conditioners), I was still lying on the floor. Today I can judge my level of comfort with a person or place by how readily I sink to the ground. At Caroline's, for example, it is a miracle that the imprint of my prone form is not embedded in her rug. When I read recently about Temple Grandin, the autistic scientist who designed and built a contraption out of wood that enclosed her on all sides, pressed into her flesh like a skintight casket, my inclination to connect as much of my skin with the surface beneath me came into sharper focus still, as a now-comprehensible, Tourettic embrace. Baths, which I still take at least once a day, and more often when under duress, are the ultimate form-fitting envelope. Relaxing in hot water, I sink down to my chin, allowing all of my excess energy to dissipate before it can escape in the form of a tic, forgetting how painfully conscious I am of my physical self when only my feet are touching the ground.

When I told my parents about these connections, about Tourette's and what I'd learned from Bryant, Dr. Iager, and my new books, they had the same response: skepticism failing to conceal disbelief.

"Remember the mono," my mother pointed out. "I'm not saying this doesn't feel real, but I think you should slow down here and not be too quick to leap to conclusions." My father repeated the word as if it tasted bad: "Tourette's," he spat. "I've never even heard of it." My peers, of course, went right for the pop culture reference, asking, one after the other, "Isn't that that swearing thing from *L.A. Law?*" Nicole thought maybe she'd seen an episode of *Geraldo* on the topic; Caroline scoffed that she—if anyone—would have known if I really had a condition so rare and severe. When I refused to let up, my overwhelmed father mailed me still a third copy of *How to Get Organized,* his foolproof cure for everything but the common cold; only Alison bought the diagnosis straight-up, claiming she'd always known I was nuts. Over the phone, in his new house in Boston alone, Ben sounded tired. "Whatever," he concluded, "Call it whatever you like. Can we fix it?"

My head swam with terminology—"pure obsessional," "thinking ritualizer," "Librium," "Elavil," "maintenance of recovery"—then overflowed. Words stuck in my head and emerged at inappropriate times; in class, when asked to explain a line in an essay, I thought "endorphins, biofeedback, dopamine," and struggled to replace them with a stab at an acceptable answer. I tackled the diagnosis as only an obsessive-compulsive could, flooding the airwaves with news bulletins and pithy quotes from my slowly expanding stock of reading material. I was a zealot, a born-again, explaining to anyone who would listen that coprolalia, the technical term I'd learned for those involuntary profane outbursts, was not a diagnostic criteria for Tourette's. I took particular delight in pointing out scientific and technical details of the disorders to my father, emphasizing the involuntary nature of behaviors he'd especially criticized, such as my head twitch. From a chapter entitled "Exposing the Myths," in Shimberg's book, I read myths #3 and #7 over and over: "A person with tics could stop them if he or she really wanted to. False. A person will stop ticcing if you bring the tic to his or attention every time he or she does it. False." With my father, I became the Clarence Darrow of Tourette's defense, and he, "the primary source of tension," as I liked to call him, was a hapless witness I cut off at every attempt to participate in the trial. Or so I imagined at first. Once, after I assaulted him with case studies from my book and ran over possible treatments, he paused and said, "So you'll take some pills and then the twitching will stop?" The hope in his voice was a left hook to the stomach. Back to square one.

It is a challenge to make people understand the nuances of a condition that is both so internalized and easy to disguise and keep secret, in its milder forms at least, harder still to get them to apply such ominous-sounding terms to someone they know, someone like me, someone who's managed to get along fine without knowing the terms so much as existed. In spite of (and spurred on by) the constant, unanticipated expressions of doubt and outright disbelief I received from others, I considered trying the Prozac Dr. Iager had recommended, figuring a change in me for the better could at the very least serve as positive proof that at one point, things had been worse.

I met Bryant on a Saturday morning, earlier than either of us is used to rising on weekends, as soon as we were both able to fill our identical prescriptions. He approached from the opposite direction, his gloves jammed haphazardly in his coat pockets, clutching a small brown paper bag in his wind-reddened left hand. My own little paper bag was at the bottom of my backpack, where I'd stuffed it in the elevator of my apartment building, afraid to be caught holding it out in the open. I'd watched the pharmacist wrapping it; the word "Prozac" practically leapt off the container, with its forcibly optimistic first syllable and flat finale: a two-part smack in the face.

I have never liked taking pills. I hated baby aspirin and its patronizing, inaccurate name. I must have palmed hundreds of the chalky little tablets, dissolved others in the sink, flushed days' worth down the toilet after storing them up between the mattress and the box spring. The other medications of my childhood, the sickeningly sweet decongestant Dimetapp, toxic cough syrups, and thick, pink erythromycin (I am allergic to penicillin) were liquids and therefore nearly impossible to dispose of surreptitiously. After a few bad cases of strep and years of chronic ear infections, I learned to hold the noxious spoonful in my mouth, though, deflating my cheeks to avoid detection, until my mother left the room and left me with two options: run to the bathroom, home to the ever-useful sink and toilet, or spit the offending substance out in a cup (once, even, a plant) and rinse it out later.

Although most adult medications come in "tasteless, odorless pills," I gag when I try to swallow them, often spitting them out with the coating half dissolved only to discover, the hard way, that they *do* have a taste: shockingly foul. At that time, I wouldn't take one or three pills, or five, because I didn't consume—or do—anything in odd numbers. This meant frequent under- or overdosing, unless my mother, in a suspicious frame of mind, insisted on watching me swallow. After such blessedly rare occurrences I would find something else to swallow to even things up: a Tic-Tac or a chocolate chip, even a tiny wad of paper. Eventually I grew wise enough to make the vital connection that not taking my medicine would result in ongoing pain. Severe menstrual cramps, a blinding migraine, and the removal of four impacted wisdom teeth desensitized me one by one, forced me to gulp and swill with something resembling gratitude; the wisdom teeth experience had me tossing back Percocet like candy.

By the time I got my hot hands on the Prozac, swallowing was no longer my primary concern. The introductory paragraph of the pamphlet provided by Rite Aid, my neighborhood drugstore, read: "This medication is used to treat depression and obsessive-compulsive symptoms associated with Tourette's syndrome. May cause drowsiness or dizziness. Use caution performing tasks that require alertness. Other side effects include heartburn, loss of appetite, headache, anxiety, flushing or sweating, change in sexual desire or ability. If these symptoms persist or become bothersome, inform your doctor."

All of these side effects struck me as significant, to varying degrees, and potentially far worse than "bothersome." The more I read on, the more I questioned my decision. If anyone didn't need more headaches or anxiety it was me, and I was pretty sure neither Ben nor I would be thrilled with the "change" in sexual desire, sure to be a change for the worse. And then there was the fact that I'd never been completely sold on medicating myself into sanity in the first place. I still remember the first time I heard of Prozac. It was when Elizabeth Wurtzel's controversial book *Prozac Nation* was published, and I read a review of it in the *Boston Globe*. Caroline and I talked about it over the phone, and we both agreed that the drug was a product of a narcissistic society in which people would rather pop a pill than take a good look at themselves in the mirror. "I would never take a drug that could change my personality," I had said, as always allowing no room for nuance. Mind over matter, I always told myself when I had a headache or a stomach cramp. For thousands of years people lived without pharmaceuticals, I asserted; reckless, profusive medicating was a modern luxury, and a dangerous one at that. If someday I became truly, seriously ill, I didn't want to be immune to the effects of the painkillers that could keep me going until my body's defenses prevailed. And a drug, any drug, that interfered with the brain? Asking for trouble, if you asked me. I'd take my brain part and parcel, foibles and all, for better or for worse until death did us part; after all, weren't the parts of us we didn't like just as much a part of us as those we did? It had taken some serious willpower to set this stance aside.

We walked purposefully down Broadway, Bryant assuming his customary position on my right; although we'd only known each other for a matter of weeks, I already felt totally comfortable in his presence—thanks to the force of common experience—and I'd fallen easily into his walking routine; the things we knew about each other without having to ask were precisely those things other people never seemed to understand. Our destination was the College Inn, a greasy spoon where no one we knew ate. The aspiring and cash-hungry writers of our acquaintance preferred the new coffee bar up near school, where they wouldn't be tempted by real, and therefore costly, food, or the even dingier Tom's, of *Seinfeld* fame, where the food was marginally worse but the prices marginally better. As we'd anticipated, a private back booth was free, and we slid into our respective seats, still not having exchanged a word.

"I feel like we're making a drug deal," stage-whispered Bryant, whose infinitesimal knowledge of drug deals was limited to TV police dramas, as was mine.

"Me too," I giggled nervously, motioning to a waitress and requesting two large glasses of water. "We have to do it before we eat," I said, "Or we won't do it at all. I *know* us." Bryant nodded at me over his menu and then, reluctantly, set the menu down.

"Yeah. You're right." The water arrived, and I dug my crinkled bag out from my backpack. Bryant centered his on the table in front of him.

"Is anyone watching?" I asked, as I was facing the rear wall and he had a full view of the place from his side of the booth.

He scanned the room. "Nope. Let's go." From the bags we removed clear brown plastic vials. "You didn't look, did you?" Bryant asked. "Did you open it up?"

"No," I answered, defensive. "Why? Did you?" He shook his head no. Satisfied that neither of us had betrayed the terms of the deal and previewed their container's contents, we screwed off the white tops and shook two 10-milligram pills each into our respective palms. The pills were capsule-shaped, half green and half white, with scratchy black lettering. They looked like the diet pills a friend of mine had taken in high school, years before I realized what she'd been up to, and not unlike the Tylenol sinus medication my mother bought in bulk for her frequent infections. They looked small and sad in our suddenly massive hands; I seriously doubted the capability of such pathetic little pills to alleviate a headache, let alone alter the chemistry of my brain.

After a few seconds perusing, sniffing, and shaking the

Prozac capsules, we placed them beside our glasses of water, mine, I noticed, to the left of my glass, Bryant's to the right of his. I reached across the table and moved his to the left side of his glass so it would match mine.

"Not funny," he said with a frown, returning his pills to their original location. I cupped a protective hand over mine, fearing retaliation.

"I'm sorry," I said. "I'm just nervous."

Bryant held out his hand. "Truce." We shook.

When Dr. Iager had decided that we should both try Prozac and suggested we take it together and share our experiences for moral support and the sake of comparison, Bryant and I had the same initial reaction: I'm not depressed. "I've never been depressed," I remember stressing at the time. "In fact, I'm very rarely even sad. If anything, I'm too happy most of the time. Do you have anything we could try to sober me up?"

Dr. Iager ignored me, well aware by this point that I was no '90s version of Annette Funicello from her *Beach Blanket Bingo* days. She'd already spent hours over the previous weeks reassuring me that Prozac was the most effective medication for OCD, and I'd done plenty of research on my own—in my ever-expanding personal library and in Columbia's—to back her up. But although I'd mostly gotten over my aesthetic distaste for a "designer drug" with so many unpleasant connotations, I was, when confronted with it on a personal level, terrified of its potential effects. I knew a few people on Prozac, but they took it so lightly, glibly explaining they'd been "down" or "out of it" when I asked why it had first been prescribed. I didn't want to tell my parents about it, figuring they'd jump to the same conclusion I'd made: that the doctor thought I *was* really depressed, but not strong enough yet to admit it even to myself. Maybe they'd take the suspicion one step further and decide that depression was in some way the source of my tics and compulsions, in spite of all the information I'd provided them to the contrary. And although I didn't share this with Bryant or Dr. Iager, it had occurred to me that, if released from all of my rituals—the deeply ingrained counting, sorting, hoarding, and checking that were as much a part of my life as getting dressed in the morning, eating dinner at night—I'd actually become someone else, someone who might resemble me, share defining aspects of me, but who was, when it came right down to it, not really me at all. There was a chicken-and-egg dilemma here that made me dizzy. If Prozac made me the me I was meant to be and the tics and rituals were but accessories, mere accoutrements, then that would be good. But if the tics and rituals were as much a part of me as the mole on the back of my neck, the yellow flecks in my irises, then eliminating them with the pop of a pill was an eradication of my very soul, a self-inflicted stab wound to the integrity of my character, the makeup of my molecules. Which came first? was the question, or, more specifically, which mattered more: a risky shot at salvation, or a whole-hearted embracing of the status quo?

Bryant and I decided we'd definitely notice if the medication had a negative effect on each other, if not ourselves, and agreed to Dr. Iager's plan. If Bryant became a grinning simpleton who also no longer had to walk on the right side of his companion or sit with both of his feet touching the floor or check his answering machine every ten minutes, then I, at least, would register the changes and tell him to chuck the rest of his medication in the nearest Dumpster. And if I were rendered capable of leaving my apartment without kissing my cat or ensuring that it was indeed 12:30 and not 12:31 or putting a penny in my pocket, but also became a glassy-eyed, moronic shadow of my former self, Bryant would know in a flash and guide me firmly back to a Prozac-free existence. The notion that the medication might merely reduce the frequency and intensity of some of our more time-consuming, irrational rituals, leaving us ourselves, but new and improved, didn't occur to either of us in a realistic way.

We opened our capsules into the glasses of water as we'd been instructed and drank them down. I swallowed mine in even gulps; Bryant chugged his and then placed his glass equidistant from both ends of the table. We eyed each other with a grain of suspicion.

"Well?" I finally asked. "Anything?"

Bryant considered. "Nope. And you?"

I shook my head no. We followed our Prozac cocktails with burgers and milkshakes and then headed back up Broadway, glancing periodically at each other out of the corners of our eyes for any signs of an unlikely, immediately detectable change. Bryant, of course, walked on the right.

WHEN MY GRANDFATHER WAS STILL ALIVE, before I turned fourteen, I used to make sundials at Lambert's Cove beach on our annual family vacations on Martha's Vineyard. I began by creating one sundial a day, when we first arrived at the beach in the morning. First, I would find a straight, sturdy stick, about the length of my scrawny, freckled forearm. Then came the time-consuming part—the heart and soul of the sundial-making process: selecting the stones.

Noon, three o'clock, six o'clock, and nine were large, white, smooth, perfectly round stones, just like the ones my father collected and took home in his briefcase, putting us in direct competition for the choicest offerings. The other hours had to be the same size as each other, and smaller than the white stones, but otherwise they could vary. Sometimes they were yellow, like the stones my grandmother preferred. Sometimes they were "lucky," what we called stones encircled by an unbroken white band; a really lucky stone, a keeper too good for the sundials, had double bands. Once or twice the in-between hours were marked by shells, but only if I could find enough perfect mussels or moonshines, which was rare, since I refused to use even slightly chipped or holey ones.

To find noon, I would ask someone for the correct time by their watch, and place the first two stones accordingly. The rest was eye-work, and I have a powerful eye for symmetry; my sundials were always uncannily accurate. Periodically over the course of the day I would ask the time and add minute stones, tiny thumbnail-size pebbles, really, mostly for decorative effect. The next day, without fail, the sundial would be gone, swept over by waves, but strangely—although I daily mourned the loss of inanimate objects, from the dandelions my father murdered by lawnmower to a flawless piece of fruit I thought better suited to looking at than eating—I never minded; there was always a new sundial to be built, and the task at hand absorbed any regret I may otherwise have had about the destruction of each prior creation.

When I first started taking Prozac, each day was an

encapsulated lifetime: minutes became hours, hours became years, a twenty-four-hour cycle had no discernible end. I would wake up tired and dry-mouthed from the medication, and down a couple of Cokes to caffeine myself into alertness. Suddenly everything I did, everything I thought, had a parallel analysis, directly related to my diagnosis and the medication that was supposed to be "curing" it; time creeped, if it moved at all. If I picked up six copies of a menu from our lobby from a restaurant we never frequented and brought them upstairs where they'd collect dust until Caitlin finally threw them away, I'd say, "That's OCD. That's hoarding." If I were caught engaging in a fierce twitching spell in my bedroom, when Caitlin popped in to check out an outfit in my full-length mirror I'd announce, "Hi, Cait. This is Tourette's," as if she needed a proper introduction to the unwieldy beast.

To speed up the process of healing, I tried to engage Caitlin actively in my own version of treatment, based on snippets of information provided in the *Stop Obsessing* book; Dr. Iager seemed more interested in how the Tourette's and OCD were making me feel than in tactics to eliminate them and hadn't yet referred me to specialists as she'd promised; the Columbia mental health services floor was inevitably jam-packed when I showed up to talk to her, and it was difficult to get her on the phone. I couldn't understand why my campaign with Caitlin wasn't more effective, why I couldn't reconcile myself to her assistance, but when she told me to stop when she caught me mid-twitch, as I'd requested, I'd twitch all the more, resenting her for noticing. In her mild "Amy, you're twitching" I heard grim and mocking echoes of my father's "You look crazy, your head's going to fall off if you don't just stop."

After I'd been taking the Prozac for about a month, my mother gave me one of those sets of poetry magnets that decorate refrigerators everywhere now, and I brought them back to New York. Caitlin protested mildly when I showed her, calling them "trendy," but failed to object strenuously, which I took as acquiescence. A few days passed, and I opened the little plastic box, separated the tiny tabs from each other, and placed the hundreds of words and parts of words randomly on the surface of the fridge. I figured we'd have guests over some night for dinner and they'd prove a handy conversation piece for a wayward minute or two.

The day after I put up the magnets, I had a class with Caitlin, the only one we shared, at 2:00 in the afternoon. At noon she returned from a meeting to make lunch and found me kneeling on the floor, one hand supporting my back, arranging the magnets in poems.

"Amy," she said with a warning tone I recognized all too well. Caitlin had recently declared that she was becoming "fluent in Tourette's," after explaining to an offended dinner guest that I wasn't ignoring her question but would answer as soon as I'd finished my twitch.

I smiled weakly. "They rhyme," I offered, in lieu of an explanation, and she obligingly read a few of the poems, praising an especially clever couplet, contributing a few of her own. At a quarter to two, she packed up her books, collected an apple and a soda from the fridge (I backed up on my knees to give her access), and removed her green suede jacket from the coat closet.

"Well?" she said. I looked at her standing expectantly by the door, bag slung across one shoulder, tapping her foot with impatience. I considered. We'd read Italo Calvino for class that week, and I'd been surprised by how much I'd loved it, had been looking forward to the class discussion all week. But I'd only incorporated half of the magnets. I'd been kneeling on the tiles in front of the fridge for over three hours, having decided halfway through the process that all of the poems had to rhyme—a particular challenge, as the magnets had not been designed with this goal in mind. Slowly I shook my head.

"I can't," I said, avoiding her eyes, knowing exactly how she was looking at me, refusing to face head-on what we were both leaving unspoken: The Prozac wasn't working. Yet.

Caitlin slammed the door on her way out. When she returned at 4:30, I was still kneeling, almost finished, still supporting my back with my hand.

"I'm almost done," I told her.

"You missed a great class," she said.

For the rest of that year people would ask us how long it had taken to sort all the words into so many perfect little poems. We'd both shrug.

I was pretty sure the Prozac wasn't going to be working any miracles for me. I took it at night, before I went to bed, as Dr. Iager had told me to, and in the morning I'd wake up foggy and parched. The taking of the pills themselves soon became a ritual; I used a particular glass, opened the capsules at ten on the dot, and swallowed each glassful in six evenly paced gulps. Then I washed the glass immediately with scalding water and a dime-size dollop of detergent, and set it to dry for the next day's use. Sometimes I thought I felt more tired than usual during the day, and a couple of times I woke up suddenly in the middle of the night, instantly alert and unable to fall back asleep. Otherwise I noticed no changes in my rituals or tics; although I knew the Prozac had been prescribed to target OCD, I still held out hope it would have a toning-down effect on the Tourettic tics most related to compulsions, such as touching things, like cracks in the sidewalk and bricks in walls.

When I complained, Dr. Iager told me to be patient, that it took months, sometimes, for Prozac to kick in, and that there were no guarantees it would work for me anyway: I should prepare myself for possible failure, in which case I could try something else. I wanted to up my dosage—sick of the wait—but she insisted on making sure I wasn't going to have any adverse side effects first, and that would take more time. I stuck to the 20 milligrams and kept waiting. And counting and tapping and sorting and twitching. And only every so often, through a low-lying cloud of my own devising, it struck me that the well-intentioned Dr. Iager, my free Columbia counseling, and a daily dose of Prozac were not really what I was waiting for.

Waiting for medicine to kick in, whether it's aspirin when you have a headache or something far less immediate (like Prozac), is like watching a plant grow. My mother had given me some paperwhites for Christmas, and one day when Caitlin was out, I set up the little glass box with the smooth black stones and the three flaking bulbs and poured in water just past the fledgling roots. I set the box in a dark, cool corner, as per the instructions that had accompanied the gift, and left to get a cup of coffee and run a few errands: post office, bank, dry cleaner's, corner store for soda. When I returned, less than an hour later, the inch-long green shoots I left behind were notably, significantly longer; the bulbs had sucked up a good half inch of the water, the level of which had visibly lowered. I moved the glass box to my desk and planted myself in front of it, prepared to wait all day if I had to, but nothing happened. The next morning each shoot was as long as my hand: the sheer perversity of nature.

Change is much easier to track in a plant than a person. When the ivy hanging in our sunniest window starts dropping brownish leaves, forcing me to lop off half the drying branches, the plant looks sick and ashamed, naked, even, against its will. When my obsessions and compulsions churn beneath my thin veneer of skin, I show no outward signs of the inward stress, or at least none that most people would see. Prozac stubbornly refused to cough up clues for months. Some days I would glide through my day in what I imagined was a normal fashion, accomplishing tasks, recording cash withdrawals in my checkbook, arriving on time for an appointment with a professor, meeting a friend for lunch at the designated restaurant with my wallet and, shock of all shocks, the book she'd asked to borrow weeks before. At first I attributed each smooth day, every activity begun and completed, to the medication. Bad days were just as much a source of finger-pointing, though, and when the four walls of my bedroom closed in on me, and I sat in the middle of my hospital-cornered bed recording lists of the activities I was supposed to be doing if I were actually able to leave the apartment, Prozac was to blame, its inefficacy or its downright wrongdoing, I wasn't sure which.

In a way, the fact that Prozac refused to be pinned down at first, to take a stand one way or another, was reassuring, fed into the lure of sameness I hummed like a lullaby. On the other hand, I was disillusioned. How dare it set me up for failure, promise the world and deliver nothing more than fatigue and a numbing of desire. I imagined a conspiracy by the pharmaceutical companies. People were so ignorant, they'd buy happiness pills if you marketed them right; in fact, what was Prozac if not a so-called happy pill that certainly didn't make me very happy, didn't live up to expectations more than sporadically? A short-order solution to a gourmet problem, that's what it was. And it wasn't enough.

eight ———

COMING *to* TERMS

Dr. Ira Feirstein's office is on the Upper East Side, in an upscale residential neighborhood I would otherwise have no reason to frequent. When I finally wrested my referrals from Dr. Iager, I called him first—figuring I'd take on my tics while I geared up for the behavioral therapy, which seemed far less concrete and might possibly even involve new-agey, self-help techniques of the genre I especially detest. Dr. Feirstein was first and foremost, in my mind, a doctor, a medical doctor, a *real* doctor, who was bound to have framed degrees from major universities lining his office walls, glowing references from socially acceptable, law-abiding lunatics, if I was so inclined to ask for them. I found my way to the formal doorway of a luxury high-rise, where a uniformed doorman gave me a sympathetic smile when I told him whom I had come there to see.

The waiting room provided no clues. Like the first psychiatrist's office I visited outside of Boston, it had a better class of magazines than the average orthodontist's, but otherwise its neutral carpeting and bland impressionist prints smacked of generic office space, and there were no other patients to measure myself against or feel superior to. Was I a patient? A client? A guest? I flipped through the previous week's *New Yorker,* which I had at home and had already read, until the door opened and a slight, serious-looking man poked his head through.

"Amy? Is that you?" His voice sounded gentler in person than it had over the phone, less severe, and I followed him into his office with no time to assess my nerves.

"That's a good issue," he said, as soon as I sat down on the chair facing his, trying not to look at the analytical couch along the back wall. *"The New Yorker* you were reading." I nodded absently, noticing that his office was full of books; one wall was lined with them from ceiling to floor, and they were stacked in towers on his desk and the side table by his chair. I spotted the telltale pink *New York Observer,* an alternative newspaper where I fact-checked occasionally for supplementary income peeking out from one pile, and tried to see if Dr. Feirstein was wearing a wedding ring; he struck me as somebody's dad, which I took as a plus.

"Do you work with many Tourette's . . . patients?" I asked, too hyperfocused to make introductory small talk or indulge in casual chit-chat. "What's your success rate?" Instead of counteracting with "I don't need your business, you little snot," as would have been appropriate, even well deserved, he pulled out a stapled packet that turned out to be my first ever issue of the Tourette Syndrome Association newsletter.

"I think you know that it's not that easy," he said, handing me the packet and placing his hands, neatly folded, on his knee. "But I also think I can help."

Dr. Feirstein had the psychiatrist's knack for conversing without revealing any personal information, but he knew how to make *me* talk and, more important, refused to blink or look away when I twitched in his office, as I did from start to finish each time, once I realized I was safe there, in the presence of total comprehension. In the face of such matter-of-factness, though, I started viewing my tics as the Tourettic equivalent of a runny nose or an itchy rash: They became symptoms, plain and simple, baggage-free, indicative of nothing more or less than Tourette's. Maybe what I really needed was a hospital—some kind of a shot.

Dr. Feirstein scoffed at this. "A person with Tourette's is like a car with an idling motor," he explained, and in my mind I became my grandmother's ancient silver Volvo: fairly reliable transportation, but perennially cranky and always in need of a tune-up. This analogy helped enable me to visualize my surplus of energy—probably dopamine, in my brain—swirling around in my body, seeking and finding its outlet in tics. Whenever I am especially twitchy today, I can almost hear my motor idle, feel it on the verge of propelling me off course smack into a wall or a tree. Once I'd stopped arriving early in an attempt to shake out the worst of the tics in his office bathroom—somehow he sensed the transition without my having to tell him—Dr. Feirstein asked me if I knew anything about the various medications used to suppress tics in those with Tourette's.

A medication called haloperidol (the brand name is Haldol) has been highly effective as a treatment for Tourette's.

Dr. Feirstein suggested starting me on half a tablet a day and building up to a livable dose. Rocking in my chair in the way that always makes me think about autism, I remembered seeing Haldol in one of the only two books I'd managed to find on Tourette's, but I couldn't place the context; when I got home I located the passage and regretted it instantly: Although Shimberg identified it as the "drug of choice" for Tourette's, she went on to exceed Rite Aid's sobering list of potential side effects for Prozac, including "fatigue, weight gain, muscle rigidity, personality changes, school phobia, skin sensitivity to light, depression, and even (although rarely) tardive dyskinesia, a condition that involves involuntary chewing-like movements and tongue thrusts." Tongue thrusts? Personality changes? Could my tottering personality tolerate any more?

I read this excerpt to Dr. Feirstein during my following session, feeling my tongue want to thrust as I did so, although I hadn't so much as received the prescription yet. With a barely concealed smile, he referred me to an essay by Oliver Sacks entitled "Witty, Ticcy Ray" for a more balanced view of the drug, as well as one man's actual experience; eventually I settled on the same stance as Ray, taking Haldol when it was important not to tic—mostly during the week—and letting my tics run rampant on weekends, when I would be twitchy and impulsive but eminently recognizable to myself and to others as well.

One day I called Dr. Feirstein and told him I would be unable to make my scheduled appointment but couldn't tell him why; later he got me to confess I'd been sorting through seventy-five dollars' worth of accumulated change, making piles of like coins totaling exactly one dollar each. "You're not taking enough Prozac," he announced. "Let's up it to forty." Eventually we settled on the 80-milligram dose I take today, and one-and-a-half tablets of Haldol, the maximum I can absorb without falling asleep standing up.

For me, once it finally took effect, Prozac was no miracle cure, brought no transcendent revelations or reversals of thought. The best explanation I can provide of its do-good-ing is that it has effectively turned down my volume, allevi-ating my tics and especially my rituals to a manageable ex-tent. Only infrequently do I fill present-day lulls with hypnotic counting, and most of the time I can make it from one place to another in a reasonable period of time; such shifts sound diminutive in scale, I know, but there's no gift quite as gratefully received as additional hours in the day. Whereas in spite of its ghastly warnings Haldol just makes me exhausted, Prozac's overriding downside is its effect not on my sex drive necessarily but on my ability to reach or-gasm. As a wedding gift to Ben and myself I stopped taking both of my medications a month before we got married in the summer of 1998 so I could fully enjoy our honeymoon and experience it—all of it—as the unadulterated me. My medication has evolved to the point of serving as a barome-ter: When I am twitchy, or preoccupied, my friends ask me if I've been skipping my Prozac; when I can't keep my head up over dinner, they know I've been taking my Haldol.

In the long run, more so than prescribing my medica-tion, Dr. Feirstein's most profound act was convincing and then helping me admit, without the humiliation and self-loathing I'd developed as a defense tactic, that I had Tourette's and OCD, the bona-fide versions, and that I was always going to have them. Constant doubting—everything from white bread versus wheat to am I ready to get married—is a distinguishing characteristic of these disorders, often preventing sufferers from accepting and following through on a diagnosis at all. After a full year of weekly sessions with Dr. Feirstein I still had not come to terms with my diagnosis to the extent that I could announce my condition in a declarative sentence; I was incapable of saying aloud, even in his office: I have Tourette's and OCD. Five times in an hour I would interrupt myself or him, with questions like "Isn't it possible that this whole thing is really just a transient childhood tic run amok?" or statements along the lines of "You know, you can tell me if this is all in my mind. I can take it. Tell me the truth—I'm making it up. I'm delusional."

"It *is* all in your mind," he agreed after that one, "but not in the way you're implying. You have to discard your own stereotypes. Remember, there's no such thing as normal."

ON THE SATURDAY MORNING before my twenty-sixth birthday—after I'd been in New York for a year and a half—Ben called to tell me out of the blue that he thought we "needed a break." We'd been acting like strangers since the summer before, when he'd asked me to marry him and I'd declined, and I suspected he'd met someone else, in Boston, while I'd been so wrapped up in myself and my transforming discoveries in New York. As it turned out, being on my own over the following year was both the worst and the best thing that could have happened to me: I missed Ben with gaping sadness, but I was completely free to focus on getting better. Craving a more casual, separate intimacy—normal male companionship of the kind I hadn't been capable of in the past, I started dating for the first time in my life, and fell into a comfortable relationship with a friend of a friend who knew nothing about my condition or fledgling treatment when we met. Sean was a smoker, and one evening, after Ben told me over the phone that his new girlfriend was moving in with him, to the house in Arlington he'd once hoped to share with me, I lit a butt Sean had left in the ashtray in my bedroom. To my total surprise, smoking, although it made me feel queasy and somehow unclean, undeniably reduced my tics. I assumed the effect was psychosomatic until Bryant and I, on the advice of a Columbia classmate, both read the essay called "A Plague of Tics" by David Sedaris in his collection *Naked*. After describing years of living with tics without ever mentioning the word Tourette's, Sedaris writes, "for some reason, my nervous habits faded about the same time I took up with cigarettes. Maybe it was coincidental or perhaps the tics retreated in the face of an adversary that, despite its health risks, is much more socially acceptable than crying out in tiny voices. Were I not smoking, I'd probably be on some sort of medication that would cost the same amount of money but deny me the accoutrements: the lighters I can thoughtlessly open and close, the ashtrays that provide me with a legitimate reason to leave my chair, and the cigarettes that calm me down while giving me something to do with my hands and mouth. It's as if I had been born to smoke, and until I realized it, my limbs were left to search for some alternative."

Backing Sedaris's claims—and Bryant's and my personal experience—is a pamphlet I recently received describing research grants from the Tourette Syndrome Association, stating that scientists are testing reports that "either systemic or intracaudate administration of nicotine potentates the cataleptic properties of haloperidol (Haldol) in rats. Open-trial clinical studies utilizing nicotine gum and transdermal nicotine patch suggest that nicotine potentates the action of neuroleptics in relieving the motor and vocal tics of Tourette's syndrome." In layman's terms, as it turns out, nicotine is a potent and natural tic suppresser; briefly I fantasized that all the smokers I knew, Sean included, also had Tourette's but kept it under wraps due to the Marlboros and Camels shooting nicotine through their bloodstreams as effectively and necessarily as a hospital IV. In reality, memories of my aunt Ruth and my longtime disdain for the habit kept me from publicly or wholeheartedly becoming a smoker, although privately I came to the conclusion that a Marlboro Light worked faster than Haldol, without the litany of debilitating side effects, and like Sedaris, I occasionally pick my poison when I need to.

When my new secret leaked out over time, Sean, who had only known me postdiagnosis, seemed genuinely interested in learning about Tourette's and OCD. An aspiring journalist, he was by nature curious; unlike Ben, who had largely ignored my tics and rituals unless they directly interfered with his life—an approach that I'd once considered ideal but that had lost allure in the light of my newfound knowledge—he asked questions, and I was at the stage when I wanted to answer them. Like Dr. Feirstein, Sean confronted my tics head-on, which helped me to do so too. When my foot moved rhythmically in bed, waking him, instead of rolling away toward the wall or sniping about it, he'd prop himself up on an elbow.

"Can you stop that?" he'd ask, not meanly, but directly, and distinctly, and I'd give the matter legitimate thought.

"No. Well, maybe yes. Let me try." He'd lie back down, placing his own warm foot over mine, pinning it gently to the mattress, and I'd concentrate hard on my foot, making it into a game, keeping it still for as long as I could, at least until Sean was soundly asleep.

When what I said or did struck Sean as odd or insensitive—for one, I talked often and openly about my lingering feelings for Ben, with whom I was realizing I wanted to make a life—he did back off, and understandably so. But I learned not to bristle when he put an affectionate arm around my shoulder or his hand on my knee in a movie theater, to let the touch sink in and settle, and will always be grateful for this desensitization to touch and honest displays of warmth by Sean, who was more physically expressive than Ben or maybe just not conditioned by me to maintain a careful distance. I will never be a spontaneous hugger, but I no longer "wipe off touches" or cringe when my skin touches someone else's skin.

Dr. Feirstein and I agreed that I needed a major diversion from obsessing over Ben. I bought *Brain Lock,* a book by UCLA psychiatrist and OCD specialist Jeffrey Schwartz, that theoretically taught readers to "change their own brain chemistry." According to well-documented studies run by Schwartz and his team, behavioral therapy, undertaken alone or in conjunction with a trained professional, was literally capable of modifying the biochemical problem that caused the brains of those with OCD to send them false messages. Apparently, making yourself break the patterns of your rituals rendered you less anxious each subsequent time you fought off the impulse. I understood the principle: I'd been trying to make myself stop doing my rituals for most of my life, but what I call the "why-not" theory always kicked in just in time to thwart my attempts. For example, it is not rational to check the mailbox on a Sunday, embarrassing to do so more than once. But when you just happen to be strolling by the box with your mail key in your pocket, and it takes only seconds to turn it in the keyhole and peer inside, why not? It doesn't make sense that if I keep my hands in my pockets for the length of a subway ride I will prevent the subway from crashing, but if it's chilly, and I don't have anything to read, and my pockets are just beckoning to be used and appreciated, why not? I even understood the faulty logic behind the "why-not," theory, and the fact that in what was effectively an inverse of behavioral therapy, the more I indulged my obsessions and compulsions, the worse they became.

I viewed behavioral therapy in the same way I viewed hypnotism. I was willing to buy that if someone believed he could be hypnotized, he could be, but I harbored no delusions that anyone would ever be able to hypnotize me, as I considered hypnotism both a pseudoscience and a fraud. I didn't question the fact that behavioral therapy had helped people with OCD change—the MRIs in *Brain Lock* provided me sufficient proof of that—but as long as I felt impervious to it, I doubted it could have any effect on me. I patiently explained all this to behavioral therapist Dr. Poller's answering machine, half hoping she'd consider my take on her profession offensive and refuse to return the call. I had vastly underestimated the banality of OCD to psychologists, who see dozens of cases a year at a minimum, many far more severe than my own. To her, I must have seemed, well, perfectly normal.

True to form, I showed up at the right building at what I was sure was our scheduled time only to face a locked office and a puzzled concierge, who told me that Dr. Poller never worked on Wednesdays, hadn't for years. *Off to a good start,* I told myself, out of synch for the hundredth time that week—*way to show I really did need help.* When I returned home after a three-hour walk and yet another wasted afternoon, I unearthed a scrap of paper in the kitchen on which I'd scrawled: BTT, for "behavioral therapy Tuesday." I showed up the following Tuesday right on time, but Dr. Poller didn't seem that surprised by my gaffe, or annoyed, as I'd feared. In fact, she looked totally disinterested when I launched into my rehearsed apology for inconveniencing her, as if she'd heard the same speech so many times it bored her to tears (a reaction I know all too well, as Caroline has perfected it to a science). Finally I stopped, to our mutual relief.

I had, astonishingly, remembered the blank notebook Dr. Poller had asked me to bring along, and I sat with it open on my lap, remembering all of the first days of school when I'd felt hopeful that the sheer newness—classrooms, teachers, school supplies, empty, expectant pages—would somehow make this year different from all the others before it. I looked up; Dr. Poller was watching my foot. I'd been trying not to twitch, but my right leg was doing its mechanical vibrating in spite of my concerted efforts. I'd always been a foot-tapper, but with a measure of control over the taps. This motion was different: I would become suddenly aware that my leg, and therefore my foot, was moving on its own, the way my teeth chattered when I was cold. Then, I could freeze the muscles in my jaw and stop shivering for a minute or two, but as soon as I relaxed my face the chattering would start up again, slowly at first, and then stronger than before, just like the leg.

I looked up from my leg and met Dr. Poller's eye. "Hmmm," she said, and that was all for then, although I eventually discovered that crossing the offending leg over the quiet one helped me keep still. Although I've never been able to keep a diary, to this day I still read my therapy journal over and over, memorizing passages like a favorite poem or song. Dr. Poller's language was accessible, not clinical, and, like Dr. Feirstein's, delivered in a tone that eliminated all my fears of feeling like a freak. "An obsession," and I quote Dr. Poller from the first entry in my journal, is "a thought that hits you suddenly and generates a lot of anxiety quickly, along with a need to alleviate the anxiety." I zoomed in on my obsessions, which suddenly struck me as manageable bundles, no longer spreading puddles in a never-ending pounding rainstorm. A compulsion was "the quick fix" for the obsession; in my head I translated an example. Tapping a manhole cover twice with my right foot on the way home from work meant not getting mugged. Obsession: Being attacked, murdered, coming to personal harm, dying. Compulsion: Tapping the manhole cover with my foot.

At the end of our first hour together, Dr. Poller announced that she would be giving me weekly homework assignments. I immediately began contriving to cancel all forthcoming sessions without having to tell Dr. Poller this to her face; the last thing I needed was more work. I was having enough trouble fulfilling my professional obligations, let alone the most rudimentary requirements of daily life, such as doing my laundry, paying my bills, and returning essential phone calls. My mouth dropped open when she explained what it was: to bring in and show her all the scraps of paper I accumulated over the following week.

How did Dr. Poller know about my "scrap principle"? Had she snooped in my bag when I'd gone to the bathroom and noticed I was at the ugly end of a hoarding cycle? I didn't care; gathering scraps was the opposite of homework— I figured I couldn't have been given a project that would require less attention or thought. Over the next week, however, the act of accumulation rose to the forefront of my daily activities, became an active process in itself, or rather the rejection of it did. For the first time in my life I spent more time worrying about *why* I was picking up gum wrappers on the sidewalk and "rescuing" discarded catalogs for menswear or beer-of-the-month clubs than about the obsessions I was trying to negate by taking them home in the first place. Every time I shoved my hand in my coat pocket in search of a movie-ticket stub on which to jot down a phone number, I felt vaguely guilty and then angry about the guilt; when I described the results of my efforts to Dr. Poller, she said that if guilt were enough to "cure" OCD, then the disorder wouldn't exist in the first place. She said my very normal discomfort meant that I'd already begun to get better.

The night after my third or fourth session with Dr. Poller, I walked straight out of a movie theater onto the street without waiting to read the name of the key grip for the first time in fourteen years; I haven't stayed for a movie's credits since. Over subsequent weeks I started to evaluate other behavior patterns and ask Dr. Poller directly about those that confused me—my guidelines for what fell into the category of acceptable had long since disappeared. For one, I identified garbage as a multifaceted conflict that had arisen between me and Ben when we'd been living together in Cambridge. Not so much sifting through it, which I did only in secret, but my need to be constantly monitoring it, which expressed itself as either an inability to throw it away or, more recently, an inability to stand having it in the house. "How many times each day do you take out the trash?" Dr. Poller asked. I felt my face redden, shame rise; I didn't want to say. Lately I'd been walking down to the street with the garbage can each time a single item hit the bottom with a resounding, mocking thud.

"Okay." She held up her hand. "Tell me this instead. How many times each day would you take out the trash if you *didn't* have OCD?" I was stumped. How many times a day *did* a normal person empty the garbage? Ben had always let the can fill up to the very top before taking it outside and replacing the bag; on occasion, if I wasn't around, he'd let two bags build up before the trip to the Dumpster. I wasn't sure, however, if this meant he was a slob or the normal garbage-remover I should aspire to emulate. I quizzed my friends. Caroline, who is germ-averse, takes her garbage out frequently, but she only has to drop it down a chute in the hallway. Caitlin said she'd never really thought about it, but she guessed when the bag was almost full. My parents reminded me they had a trash-masher, which—I remembered then—my father monitored like a one-man sanitation department. Factoring in all this, I decided that, to start, once every two days would suffice, and Dr. Poller concurred. Progress—wars are won battle by battle.

We established more rules, and each replaced a

nonproductive ritual or compulsion. I was to pay my bills on the first and fifteenth of every month, and when they came into the house I was to place them immediately in a cigar box reserved specifically for their storage. When I was writing, I assigned myself breaks: Write for fifteen minutes, do dishes for five. Write, fifteen, go out for soda, five. Dr. Poller thought it essential that I learn to distinguish my brain's false messages from its real ones and explained the crucial distinction we with OCD persistently fail to make on our own: the world of difference between an intention, of which I had an infinite number, and a decision, of which I made none, a state that left me as reliable as New England weather in spring. Most of the time, when I said I was going to do something—from meeting Caroline for dinner to completing a freelance editing project—I avoided making a real decision to do so in fear of reducing my options, feeling locked in; apparently, other people's brains regulated this process for them, allowing them to follow through. I was going to have to create the missing structures in mine virtually from scratch.

With Dr. Poller's guidance, instead of recording important dates and meetings on scraps of paper, I struggled to keep an appointment book, and I do mean struggled. I placed time-sensitive papers such as parking tickets inside, so I'd know where they were on my prescheduled payment dates. When I made plans with friends, or with Sean, I chose a specific time, as opposed to my favorite "Maybe I'll drop by later," which usually resulted in a last-minute phone call canceling the get-together under the premise that we'd never really had an actual plan. I took my Haldol before potentially stressful social situations in the name of salvaging friendships and visualized myself without OCD when I otherwise would have been feeling sick over what I was meant to be doing but wasn't, which had become an active, all-consuming process—twenty-four-hour-a-day damage control. As Dr. Poller pointed out when I resisted trying out these changes, "If you always do what you've always done, then you'll always get what you've always got." Sounds gimmicky I'm the first to admit, but I couldn't argue with the results. When my frequent slip-ups occurred, I tried hard to suppress feelings of failure and inadequacy and instead repeated the mantra she'd told me to use at such times, although I'd told myself I'd never even think it on first hearing: It's not me, it's my OCD.

BRYANT, recently finished with the Columbia writing program and lacking inclusive health insurance, is not taking Haldol and does not go to behavioral therapy, but I share my lessons with him and force him, whenever I can, to break the molds of his compulsions. Sometimes I worry that the allowances we unconsciously make for each other though, now that I know what they are, are actually detrimental to our progress, as we tend to naturally indulge each other's compulsions in a way most of our other friends do not. During bad spells now I avoid going certain places with him, such as the grocery store; we're both capable of agonizing for an hour over which brand of paper towels to buy, as if the day's success or failure rides on the decision. We are equally ill-equipped to make decisions of any kind, in fact—often we resort to a premeal phone call to a mutual friend and ask him or her to tell us where we should eat, a practice Dr. Poller once called a cop-out and a crutch.

One night, when no one was answering the phone, we set off on our own. Rejecting one restaurant as too expensive, another as too generic, we finally reached one I'd been wanting to try for a while. I stopped in front of the menu posted in the window. Bryant nodded.

"This looks okay," he said, surprised, as I was, that we'd managed to settle on a place so quickly, before either of us had grown so hungry that we'd be forced to go home and eat something from my fridge, which had happened often enough in the past. Bryant pushed open the heavy door, and an unwitting hostess told us to seat ourselves. It was early for dinner in New York, and the place was pretty empty; a few couples sipped wine and poked listlessly at equally listless salads in the back, near the kitchen. We selected a table in the window with prime sidewalk views, and I took the seat in the corner. After I'd shrugged off my coat and settled in, I realized that Bryant was still standing, coat on, blinking furiously.

"Oh, no," I said. "Not this time. I'm starving."

"Come on," Bryant pleaded. "You can have next time."

"I've heard that before," I said. "We're leaving." There was no way I could sit in the other seat. I'd chosen mine, decided on it, and now that I'd sat in it, there was no way I'd reverse the decision. I entertained the idea for a moment, but it was too late; the seat had become mine, felt right, simply could not be abandoned. As we walked by her on our way out, the hostess frowned.

"Something wrong?" she asked, not looking terribly concerned.

"Oh, no. We're just crazy," I said, the words spewing forth from some buried recess, causing us both to erupt in laughter. We laughed all the way back to my apartment where fortunately half a leftover pizza sat on the bottom shelf of the fridge.

Not all the time, not even most of the time, but often enough that it is a source of irritation to others, Bryant or I will decide that we have to sit in a particular seat, use a particular mug, wear a particular jacket, even if it's on someone else at the time. It is not just that we "feel like it"—although that is part of it—it is that we are convinced, in spite of our capacity for logic and judgment, that something bad will happen if we don't. There is never, in fact, any logic behind these arbitrary decisions; it's not about the better view, more comfortable chair, or anything we could ever explain.

Walking down a street with Bryant is like performing a complex pas de deux. As a former dancer, I learn easily the intricacies of moving with a new partner, the minute shifts and fine-tuned awareness that are required in order to create an effortless whole. If I want to torture Bryant, I will wait until he's engrossed in a conversation or train of thought while we're walking and then subtly slip over to his right side. It grates on him like nothing else when he realizes he's been walking, even for just a few feet, on the "wrong" one.

When I have a throat twitch, am clicking my teeth or sniffing or clearing my throat, Bryant is the only person who does not attempt to finish my sentences for me. When my twitching is especially bad, as it is less and less, it is Bryant I call, and I can't count the times he continues to leave me what would be to anyone else a cryptic message: Tics are bad; call ASAP.

nine ————————————————————

THE GIFT *that* KEEPS *on* GIVING

The only science class I took in college was a biology lecture that may as well have been called "Hitting the High Points for English Majors Who Will Never Go to Medical School." I signed up partly under pressure from my friend Dana, also an English major but one with a bent for self-improvement, and partly because the course catalog promised that a third of the class would be devoted to genetic engineering. My old friend Mendel, I thought, who predicted the future and pulled children, perfectly formed and blue- or brown-eyed as announced in advance, from a double helix-shaped hat. The rational aspects of genetics have always appealed to me, the "if/then" statements the subject lends itself to so neatly, but so does the possibility of surprise, the fact that Mendel, and anyone else who tells you your child is going to be short or blond or diabetic or anything else, can't be entirely sure. I think this is somehow related to my personal version of religion, but then, it was also linked to the investigative work my subconscious was undertaking largely on its own.

Our birthday cards from my Bubby, my father's mother, were always heavier than the rest of the cards in the mailbox. We opened them first—brightly colored elephants or clowns spotted with dimes and an occasional quarter, each tucked neatly in its own little slot. After a while we took the coins out and put them away in our zippered change purses, rich and anticipatory. Without the dimes, the cards looked wilted: the clowns depressed, the elephants droopy. We'd prop them up behind the others displayed on the mantel, the slits conspicuous like gashes.

For most of my life Bubby lived at Musketaquid Village, an assisted-living facility for the elderly in Sudbury, just a mile up the road from where my mother's parents—Mormor and Papa—lived, and where Mormor still lives today. Every other Sunday at lunchtime my father would drop us off in front of her apartment, parking his expensive car illegally just outside the front door while he came in to say hello. At Bubby's we ate things we did not eat at home: moist and salty chicken legs, bagels with melted American cheese, Jell-O with fake whipped cream—the kind my mother said was 100 percent chemicals, no cream—and melt-in-your-mouth canned green beans. We could eat as much as we wanted of whatever we wanted but we could never eat enough to satisfy Bubby. She wanted to know what on earth my mother was feeding us at home. My mother wanted to know why we would only eat green beans that came in a can.

In every way, Bubby's apartment was very different from my house but not unlike my father's office, which he had been allowed to decorate and furnish himself—in black, red, and white, with geometric furniture and no rounded edges or decorative flourishes—and in which my mother rarely set foot if she could avoid it. Small but impeccably ordered, everything was always in exactly the same place, creating a sense of timelessness, or maybe stagnancy, that made me feel at home. All the food that did not need to be refrigerated was kept in a white metal cabinet in the living room, each shelf organized by product. "Now there's a woman with too much time on her hands," my mother would say to us on the way home after her rare visits. The chairs in the living room were covered in heavy plastic, as was the long low sofa that stood against the wall behind a small coffee table. A blue glass jar filled with butterscotch candies sat square in the middle of the coffee table. The level of the candies never varied; I always checked.

When Bubby had a heart attack, she managed to get to the emergency switch in her bathroom; it was only the second time the switch had ever been used. The telephone rang at our house at five in the morning and woke me up. I padded downstairs in the dark, but my father, already dressed, told me to go back to sleep, and he shut the front door carefully and silently behind him. My aunt Sheila, who lives on Mount Desert Island in Maine, caught the first plane out of Bar Harbor. My mother took the day off and fought traffic to meet her at the airport. They reached the hospital just in time to say good-bye.

The day after the funeral we went to clean out the apartment. The lock stuck when my dad tried to open it; as he jiggled the key I noticed a face in a window across the courtyard watching us from behind the corner of a curtain. When we filed in, everything looked so familiar I half expected Bubby to appear in her "housecoat" with a platter of bagels; there were no indications that anything had been moved or disturbed. I had never before been in the apartment without having something to eat, but I felt funny even taking a butterscotch. The bride doll—a bingo prize I had coveted for years, the green leather jewelry chest that clicked open when you pressed the latch, the oatmeal carton filled with our crayons, the decks of cards worn soft from years of use—everything was exactly where it was supposed to be, where it had always been. In the closet, each item was wrapped individually in layers of tissue paper and fastened tight with elastic bands. On the kitchen counter and bureau and bedside tables, each object sat deliberately at right angles to the nearest straight edge. After a respectful pause, we separated and dug in. Five minutes later my father was sprawled on the plastic-covered couch looking through old photographs, my aunt was on the telephone to Maine, and Alison and I were trying on costume jewelry in front of the mirror in the bathroom.

My eight-year-old cousin Brook shouted from the bedroom. She had found a twenty-dollar bill wedged between the wall and a picture of my father at ten sitting on a horse and wearing a cowboy costume that hung above the bed. "Lucky you." My aunt smiled at Brook. "She must have stored it there for emergencies." The halfhearted piling and sorting started up again. A few minutes later Alison shrieked from the kitchen.

"I found one too!" Hers was under the base of the blender.

My aunt shrugged and looked at my father, eyebrows raised. "I hadn't realized she was getting so absentminded."

"She wasn't," my father said, an uncustomary edge in his voice. "Dr. Brown told me she was perfectly sharp."

A few minutes later my father found a twenty rolled up in a box of Band-Aids he had opened after cutting his finger removing the plastic sofa cover, and that was that. The apartment was infested: mostly twenties and an occasional ten. They came faster and faster, tucked in the folds of a silky slip, under the base of a lamp, between the mattress and the box spring—my own favorite hiding place at home. It became a treasure hunt, the shrieks more frenetic with each find. We found hundreds of bills, maybe more. I never learned the total amount.

"Why did Bubby hide her money? Didn't she have a bank account?" At five, Ethan had recently opened his own bank account and was learning about the stock market. We were sitting in the aftermath on the exposed sofa and chairs, the treasure hunt over, the money, to the best of our knowledge, found. No one answered Ethan, and Alison asked the question that was on the minds of all present under the age of forty: Do we get to keep what we found? My aunt and father exchanged a long look; my father looked away first.

"Uncle Joel will take the money to the bank," my aunt said firmly. "I think it's time to leave."

How far back does this cycle go? Is obsessive-compulsive behavior a quirk of the system—green eyes? long second toes? a cleft palate or port wine stain of the brain?—trickling down family trees like water dosed with cyanide? My father's father, from all accounts a mild-mannered, kind, but wishy-washy man, died young, in his early sixties. My dad and my aunt don't remember him having a rigid or compulsive bone in his body. Bubby, however, who lived five minutes down the street from us for much of my life, was a living emblem of rigidity and compulsion, not to mention her obsessions with health and cleanliness, enslavement to patterns of organization, countless anxieties and crippling resistance to change; she lived eighty years without ever learning to drive, never venturing farther from home than Atlantic City, or Maine, to visit my aunt, Brook, and Ethan. Although she told us so little about herself, Bubby—because she literally couldn't stop herself—left sufficient clues behind to target her as a solid link in this chain of ritualized behavior.

In some ways, my father is his mother's son times ten. In the twenty-five years he has owned his own business, he has followed the same schedule to the minute regardless of weather condition, illness, crisis, or fatigue, although he works alone with no colleagues to impress with his infallible punctuality. Like me, but with tremendous pride in and fear of veering from his powers of efficiency, he follows inflexible rules for every move he makes, from setting his alarm clock each night to timing his shower each morning and parking his car in the driveway upon returning home from an errand or work. At his office, as at home, he devotes what amounts to hours consumed with thoughts of the status of the front door, which must be locked at all times, even when he walks fifty feet around the side of the house to get the mail, and the lights, which must be off, unless the house will be empty for a while, in which case they all—and the stereo—must be on, loud and blazing, in my mind a certain beacon to Sudbury's surely minuscule population of roving bandits that no one, not even an insect, is in the house: What living creature, after all, could tolerate such unforgiving light, such glaring sound?

He structures his leisure time, too, even on the rare

occasions when planned activities are not recorded on the monthly calendar, which has rested, folded open, on the same spot of our kitchen counter for two decades now and is replaced each December with a new model, leaving us all with more than enough time to make the transition to the new year. He plays basketball on weekdays, from 11:30 to 1:30; even as a very young child I knew precisely where to find my dad at any given minute of the day, and his schedule has varied little, if at all, over the course of my life. In the evenings he reads or watches sports, usually basketball, keeping track of the NBA and NCAA team records down to the lifetime stats of the benchwarmers; he claims to have only a passing interest in football and baseball, but I've never seen him stumped by the most minute details of the history or present-day leagues of either sport, on the college or professional level. When he accidentally saw the movie *Wings of the Dove* and reported to me he'd found it "slow," with an "implausible" storyline, I asked him if he'd ever even heard of Henry James.

"Sure," he said, clearly unsure as to the relevance of the question. "He was a left-handed point guard at North Carolina State in 1970-something, good playmaker, I'll let you know what year. I've got it in one of my books."

My mother often wonders what great thoughts and plans could otherwise occupy the space in a brain that so fiercely stocks up such wealths of trivia, hones in on such irrelevant detail. "Is that important, Joel?" she asks frequently when he identifies songs on an oldies' station one after another for hours at a time or lists every movie John Wayne ever made, in order and by accurate name. As a toddler, I used to copy him and memorize the professional basketball rosters, checking myself against my dad's yearly NBA guides and back issues of *Street & Smith* magazine, which were updated by him biweekly as to trades, retirements, and recent acquisitions, with modifications highlighted and color-coded for instant accessibility. I may well have been the only four-year-old girl in the country who could recite the entire roster of the 1974 Washington Bullets.

After just a few weeks of treatment, Dr. Feirstein and Dr. Poller both pointed out how frequently my father crept into our discussion, both as a source of comparison and a means of creating contrast. Finally, tentatively, Dr. Feirstein took an opportunity when I stopped for breath in the middle of describing my father's extensive personal mailing lists, which he uses primarily to distribute family ephemera of virtually no interest to others, and asked, "Has it ever occurred to you that your father might have OCD?"

This stopped me in my tracks. "My mother says he's a 'Type A' personality," I said, but come to think of it, I hadn't heard that term tossed around much of late, hadn't seen it in any of the up-to-date materials I'd been scouring over the past few years. And I'd always thought my father's mode of living was much more than just uptight; it's not his personality that's so rigid, it's the rules and regulations he's constricted by. I cocked my head, considering, wondering if acknowledging the possibility would be to open a long-sealed can of worms. "I guess it's occurred to you," I said then, and he nodded, with his "Bingo" expression.

"Why don't you talk to Dr. Poller about this," he said, and I agreed. On the subway ride home, I thrilled to the prospect. It seemed outrageous not to have come to this conclusion earlier, immediately even, on my own, but the manifestations of his obsessive-compulsive behaviors were so diametrically opposed to mine in so many ways that the connection—now so painfully obvious—had totally escaped me. At the request of Dr. Poller, I called my dad and asked him to make and send me a list of the things he felt he "must do," and the reasons why, without explaining the purpose. An inveterate list-maker, he obliged unquestioningly and faxed the long list to me later that very day. I didn't need to show it to anyone else for confirmation, and I thought for an instant about filing it away and never referring to it again. People without OCD did not drive back and forth from home to the office more than once to make sure the copy machine was turned off, the first item on his list. To begin with, they knew that leaving a copy machine on overnight poses about as much threat of danger as a rubber plant. They didn't pull the car over to the side of the road, physically unable to drive, if an object such as a coin or a Post-it note was resting on the dashboard. Most likely, they wouldn't even notice. They didn't regularly prowl the house at odd hours checking the light switches, flicking each one off and on a predetermined number of times, or count the number of ice cubes in the cat's water several times each day, or become visibly agitated when forced to park just inches away from their "regular spot" in their own driveway; by no means did they admonish the wife or daughter who inadvertently infringed upon their designated patch of gravel. They certainly didn't time the length of their showers or record the message on their answering machine over and over again, in search of the "just right" pitch and tone. My father's OCD was more textbook than mine.

The next day, unrequested, another list slid out of my fax

machine, this one listing his childhood compulsions, some of which I knew about already but had never bothered to analyze, such as the treasured, professional-quality stamp collection I'd been allowed to peruse as a child and had taken away when I couldn't adhere to "the system," and the hundreds of numbered comic books his mother had thrown out when he left home for college, an act for which he'd never forgiven her. His record collection was impossibly complete, his knowledge of the rock groups of the 1950s and 1960s unparalleled; apparently his baseball card collection had been the envy of his neighborhood, and he had been famously capable of locating any one of the thousands of cards in seconds, due to a complex organizing system of his own devising. His high-school yearbook referred to him as a "meticulous dresser," and an unusual preoccupation with clothing—its color, fit, brand, and feel—has lasted through the present day; in fact, when I first got to know Bryant, I kept thinking that shopping with him reminded me of something, but I wasn't sure what. Once, watching him appraise the way a blue button-down shirt sat on his shoulders in a store mirror, I realized that only my father treated clothes with such reverence and loving care.

Today, on those occasions when my father and I are walking together, I am aware of each sidewalk crack we both step over, the way we naturally adjust our steps so they match, so the beats made by our steps don't interfere with each other and create a cacophony of aberrant taps on the pavement. Many of his habits that I remember with dread from my childhood, even those that used to drive me to tears, are emerging in me; things could be worse, I grumble in my apartment at night, pacing back and forth to the bathroom light switch, furtively searching for runaway pens, insisting that all doors and windows remain locked at all times, even if we're sitting around at home in broad daylight on a Sunday afternoon. (Better safe than sorry, I assert, unsure if I am imitating learned behaviors, or living out a genetically coded waking nightmare, or both.)

For me, my father is more than a source of constancy, a twenty-four-hour-a-day personal secretary, a one-man organizing machine without whom my attendance at any educational institution from first grade on and my own wedding would not have been possible, a nag. He is a shaping force of my OCD; throughout childhood and adolescence I rebelled not by staying out all night without calling home or wrecking the car by racing on the Massachusetts Turnpike and sliding into a guardrail, but by unconsciously shaping my own obsessions and compulsions in ways that would most violently clash with his; where he is on time, I am late, where he is fastidious, I am messy—such juxtapositions are endless but have one unerring factor in common: They are all flip sides of the same coin. Neither of us ever chooses the middle ground; we can't.

Tourette's syndrome runs in families, like hemophilia. Apparently the gene responsible can also be expressed as just OCD, which seems to be the case with my father; according to everything I have read and been told, there is a good chance my own children will have one or the other or both. When I told my mother about the genetic component, about the lists my father had been faxing me of his own volition, she rubbed her forehead with the back of one hand, rumpling her bangs in a way that always makes me fight the urge to straighten them. "I've always thought your father wasn't in control of some of his compulsive behavior," she said after some thought. "Why don't you talk to him about it? Delicately. I think he'll surprise you." So, skeptically, I broached the subject with my dad.

"Do you think it's possible that you too have OCD?" I asked when we were sacked out in his den, on his home turf, watching *A Bronx Tale* from his alphabetized video collection, while Midnight, who'd been the unwitting primary target of his obsessive-compulsive behavior since Alison and I had left home, purred contentedly between us.

"I don't do that crazy thing with my head," he said quickly, and I took a deep breath. "Wait," he added "I don't mean crazy. Just that thing with the head."

"I didn't say you had Tourette's. But *I* may have Tourette's because *you* have OCD." It was time to pull out all the stops. "I really think you should consult a psychiatrist," I said, before I could worry too much about the ramifications of the prospect or contemplate warning area mental healthcare professionals what might lay in store for them. To my amazement, he promised to think about it, but I didn't hold out much hope.

My father feels blessed to have children. Years ago he made an unspoken promise to himself to be the proverbial parent he'd always longed for as a child, and for the most part, he has succeeded beyond his own expectations. However, he did not deal well with my tics, a parenting obstacle he'd never imagined, and I wonder now if some of his intolerance and misguided anger at me was due to buried frustration with his own compulsions, which he had never dared contemplate, let alone name. He has taken the time to learn about my tics, but he still isn't quite comfortable hearing me talk about them or when I tic in his presence; his eyes don't quite meet mine, and he changes the subject if I so much as pause for breath or turn my back for an instant. It was no coincidence that my first aborted attempt at seeking treatment ended with a triumphant phone call to my father, as opposed to a follow-up consultation. For years, it was almost enough for me that *he* knew I wasn't ticcing on purpose. In the center of the vicious circle created by Tourette's, he witnessed the worst of my tics, because the level of stress I felt around him when I had the impulse to tic exacerbated their ultimate manifestation. When I re-create family dinners in my parents' dining room today, forcing myself to conjure up specific scenes, or return home for a weekend visit and assume my same-old place at the table, I feel my muscles clench, neck jerk slightly, in a familiar sobering way.

The phone rang early one morning in 1998 when I was getting ready to go out, and I had to decide whether to answer it or let the machine take the call. With a glance at my watch, I opted for the machine, until I heard my father's voice, as excited as he gets on holidays, when the entire day focuses intentionally on socially implemented and acceptable ritual, and he can undertake his regular missives like a jolly, crazy, computer-programmed elf. "I have a doctor's appointment today," he announced, and I picked up the phone.

"What kind of doctor's appointment?" I asked, and finally exhaled when he said it, with the odd sensation that I'd been holding in that bit of breath for years. My father's new psychiatrist diagnosed him after one session with a spectrum case of OCD. Like me, my father grappled with the ramifications of a diagnosis with equal measures of displeasure and relief, although his eventual acceptance of it, and subsequent treatment, may have added ten years to my mother's life. He has jumped on the OCD bandwagon and takes his own 80 milligrams of Prozac each day, occasionally calling to check if my dosage has changed or to compare side effects. "Are you tired in the afternoons, Aim?" he'll ask, "because I've been taking these mini-naps, and I'm not sure what to make of it." He has taken to sending and faxing me articles he finds on OCD in magazines and newspapers, and recently sent away for a copy of an episode of a talk show on OCD, which he sent along to me too. I have given up hope that he will be less obsessive about OCD than anything else. Last summer, as my family sat on the beach together reading, he lowered Ira Berkow's *To the Hoop,* the basketball book I had given him for Father's Day.

"You've got to read this, Amy," he called out, holding the book open dramatically now, as if giving a lecture. "It's about Elgin Baylor. Berkow says he had a 'nervous neck twitch.' Maybe Elgin Baylor had Tourette's!" Great, I thought. That should be of some help to me in daily life. But I murmured a "That's really interesting" in the name of positive reinforcement: Knowledge is preferable to harassment. My dad is finally learning, in his own methodical style, that not every twitch moves me closer to insanity; that, in fact, the tics are a by-product of a gene that is likely passed down from his side of the family. I *am* afraid that backed by his Elgin Baylor theory, he'll decide it's not too late for me to live out the dream he's long had for one of his children: to play professional basketball.

Although I see my father too sporadically to notice any posttreatment difference in his obsessive-compulsive behavior, my mother—who has been married to him for thirty-one years—finds him drastically improved. Generally, she says, he is far less rigid about his rules and his schedule and those who interfere with either. He still calls me several times a day, and on the same occasions he's always called—on the way to and from the YMCA before and after he plays basketball (purportedly to give me a prediction for and a report on his play), on his way back to Sudbury after every Celtics game, in the mornings, when he suspects I'm just awake, and in the evenings, to make sure I know what games are on TV. The advent of car and cellular phones has exacerbated his obsessive calling tendencies and provided him with twenty-four-hour access to all three of the women in his life, much to our shared dismay. But when he called one evening, pride crackling in his voice, to tell me that he'd left work, felt his usual compulsion to drive back to his office, park, trek up the stairs and check to see if he'd left the copy machine on (which, I made him confess, he hasn't done once in thirty years), and fought it, forcing himself to continue driving home instead, I felt my pent-up resentment start melting away at the edges. It's comforting to have, and know that I have, a partner in crime.

I DO NOT SHARE this distasteful truth with my father, or mother, or husband, or—up until this very moment—myself, but sometimes, when I can't be reached by drugs or the management techniques I've learned in therapy, I do not do the things I am supposed to do. I guess that seems obvious, but I don't mean things like homework and keeping appointments and paying bills and watering my plants, which I also often do not do, but in this I am far from alone. I am talking about the most rudimentary functions of a normal life, about words as elemental as sustenance, maintenance, socialization, sleep.

There are times when I forget to drink. Every couple of years or so it becomes severe; I start feeling faint and nauseous one afternoon, and think, inevitably: I am ill. Now that I am older, this is replaced with: I am pregnant, which I imagine is pretty much the same sensation. Then, after dinner, the feeling lifts, and I am fine until the following day when my head empties, my eyes blur, and I have to sit down on the stairs I am climbing or on the grimy floor of the subway I am riding or in the middle of the aisle of the bookstore I am shopping in. Occasionally I faint, a quiet faint, not a dramatic collapse, no heaving bosom, hand across the forehead, just a whisper of a faint—a removal, for an instant, of my self from space and time. Come to think of it, it happened on my honeymoon. We were walking through the center of dry and dusty Lisbon, by a newsstand, and as I ran my eyes along the rows of magazines, the unfamiliar words grew soft, then certifiably fuzzy; my legs buckled, and when Ben turned around, finally, ten paces ahead of where I crouched in a dusty, busy intersection, I didn't see him until I felt his hand on my shoulder, my clammy forehead.

"Water," he said, and literally willed me to a safer corner of the sidewalk, where he made me drink an entire bottle of spring water and then half of another. "You're totally dehydrated. When's the last time you had water?" I still couldn't speak, couldn't quite get a hold of my voice, so it didn't occur to me that I'd never told him this before, that this had happened before, that I had gone weeks without water sometimes, periodically rediscovered it as a beverage option and wondered like a child why I didn't drink it always when it tasted so clean, so clear.

Other times I forget to eat or, more specifically, to notice what I'm eating. I can go for days on a single food, preferably something from a box or a bag, a foodstuff in units, making it easy to count: six cookies for breakfast, six cookies for lunch, six cookies for dinner. When I lived with Caitlin, for over a week I ate only Chex mix that I made every four days and hid in a large plastic tub under my bed; I ate it in bed, counting the little cereal grids, four at a time, two at time, never just one, never a handful.

I am saving the worst for last: Drinking and eating are complicated for more people than not, in a whole host of debilitating ways. In the bathroom one morning my red toothbrush fell into my line of vision: teeth, I thought. Toothbrush, toothpaste, teeth. I brushed my teeth, and my gums bled red, like the toothbrush: When is the last time I did this? I thought, licking the blood from my pleasingly sore gums, watching it drip into the sink, then leak out around the edges of my teeth. It feels new, I thought, like water, like morning.

Although I immerse myself several times a day in water so hot Ben can't hold a finger in it, sometimes I have the same response to soap: I see its shape first and find myself thinking: rectangle, rectangle, twice, for six syllables, then green, then soap, which if you say it fast feels like breathing in a long wisp of air, sucking it down hard into the very bottom of your throat. Then I wash, scrubbing myself so hard that it's not until hours later, when my skin loses the superficial red of its temporary scalding and I notice scrapes and scratches on my arms and thighs, that I remember with approval: yes, soap. That is what soap is for.

Sometimes, for a finite chunk of time, the thought of cloaking my skin in anything but the same two items of clothing makes my head hurt. My tan corduroys are falling apart at the seams, my gray sweatshirt is threadbare, but I am a soldier, subverting my individuality for the greater good of a cause I don't fully understand, and they are my uniform. All day and all night I wear them in my apartment like armor, like bedding. Once in a while I wear them out of the house, to the grocery store or to buy the paper, and revel in the knowledge that I have pulled one over on the world at large, taken my inside-self outside for a casual promenade, am walking through the ignorant streets in my secret disguise.

The older I get, and the more arsenals I acquire, the better I get keeping my secrets, sometimes overriding them, passing for normal. For days at a time I will forget that I'm not, chalk up a few meaningless threshold taps to a good mood, an apple chomped in bites of twos a feasible stress release, a no-cause-for-alarm celebration of symmetry. The reality checks, when they hit, hit hard, leave me reeling now: Did I imagine that stare, that flinch, that grimace, or was it really meant for me?

Crossing the street on a Sunday afternoon this spring, at the 72nd Street intersection on the West Side, I feel light on my feet and in my head. I am shopping, coming from the shoe store, headed for Fairway, where I will buy groceries to make a complicated, stress-relieving dinner, to which I plan to invite a few friends, Caroline and Mindy, definitely, maybe Nicole, although I'm pretty sure she's out of town.

Ann is in D.C.; I count her out for this one. I wonder what Greg is doing; these are such good Sunday thoughts: food and friends, fresh air and new clean shiny shoes, and I smile at the woman walking toward me, the young woman in exercise clothes pushing a stroller, in which I detect the hint of a baby, just the top of a head bared to the air. The woman smiles too; we are two young women, not yet thirty, in different phases of our lives, but content with our choices and appreciative of each other's. Then, as we near, in an instant the length of a snap of the fingers, I see her smile change, as slow as plants grow, as surely as the transformation into spring. A deformation, really—I watch, transfixed, her mouth contort, shift from upturned then to open then to flat and broken, like a flimsy, child's bicycle underneath the wheel of an eighteen-wheeler truck. I am twitching, I realize then, am in the middle of a twitch, and I know before I feel it. My head is angled up and out, my eyes are to the right—I see the sky, the top of the Apple Bank building, the awnings of the market up the street, all at a slant that makes this patch of city magic, and I question, as the woman's face turns blank, as she turns away, passes by with her hidden child, whose perception has been altered, what has really transpired in the instant of exchange.

Let me say this, in honor of all of the people I walk by and judge or ignore, all those I flatter and admire and demean and belittle and aggrandize and presume to know like all you too, because this is the nature of people, whatever our story, whatever we claim. Let me say this, and then it can rest: Have you ever stood on a street corner somewhere on one of those gentle winter days that make weathermen smile self-congratulatory smiles on every morning newscast as if they'd conjured the sunshine expressly for you, unfastening the heavy wool coat that suddenly feels much too warm, unnecessarily bulky, and looked up at the cloud wisps, swirling off blithely in one direction or another, rushing westward, clumping and dividing, like mercury, or heavy cream in a hand-hot cup of coffee, and wondered to yourself, for not the first time, about the relationship between the sky and the ground beneath your feet? Have you ever stopped, standing there, oblivious to the strangers passing by, the children calling, taxis honking, sirens blasting, and asked yourself, just because the question occurs to you, which is really in motion, the earth or the air, and why you should believe what we're told from as early as we can be made to believe it: that the earth is spinning, yes, but that the clouds move too?

AFTERWORD

Samuel Johnson, the author of the English language's first dictionary and the college seminar classic *The Lives of the Poets,* picked at his cuticles until they bled, consistently touched every fencepost in his line of vision, and engaged in a complex routine of steps each time he crossed over a threshold. Many experts, including Oliver Sacks, say today he'd certainly be diagnosed with Tourette's. Although the evidence is less convincing, according to several of his biographers Mozart suffered from violent mood swings, full-body tics, irrational impulses, and a love for nonsense words, and was often seen spinning, leaping, and fidgeting. When the *British Medical Journal* published a controversial article by a renowned endocrinologist speculating that Mozart may have had Tourette's, papers from *New York Newsday* to the *Los Angeles Daily News* followed up on the story. And Howard Hughes, Hollywood producer, world-class aviator, and billionaire entrepreneur, was terrified of germs for much of his life and refused to touch door handles, expose his skin to sunlight, and eat food that had not been specially prepared by gloved aides trained for the purpose. Although he earned his reputation as an eccentric recluse, there is little doubt he was a victim of a severe manifestation of OCD.

At the tail end of the twentieth century, Tourette's and OCD are no longer alien terms to most people, but misconceptions abound, and around the world—even under the privileged circumstances in which I was raised—the disorders still go widely, shockingly, undiagnosed. Many sufferers, such as me, Bryant, and most of the men and women I've met through the Tourette Syndrome Association, failed to receive any explanation for their crippling tics and behaviors until well into adulthood.

A few celebrities are doing what they can to draw attention to Tourette's. Jim Eisenreich, a professional baseball player most recently with the Florida Marlins, showed symptoms of Tourette's at the age of six but was not diagnosed until twenty-three; since that time he has worked with the TSA and other charities to attract attention to the disorder and much-needed funds for research. Another phenomenal athlete, Mahmoud Abdul-Rauf (the former Chris Jackson), currently playing professional basketball in Europe, was best known here for his frenetic style of play and on-court tics and compulsions; he was diagnosed with Tourette's at seventeen, years after he'd discovered his skills as a ballplayer. In childhood, he was prescribed medication for epilepsy and misled to believe that his tics were caused by an accidental bang on the head. Although these men have done much to make the world aware of Tourette's, clearly much more still needs to be done.

There are no cures for Tourette's and OCD, which are both considered lifelong disorders, although, as you've seen, they can be controlled quite effectively in many cases with a combination of medical and behavioral therapy. More disconcertingly, the medical community does not know the origins of Tourette's or OCD, or the exact nature of their relationship, beyond its certitude that there is a genetic, inherited component to both. What *is* for sure is that as more and more children are diagnosed with one or the other or both, parents will began to demand answers to the infinite number of questions these disorders raise, separately and as a particularly debilitating team.

In the last few years, research has conclusively shown that there is some kind of a link between group A Beta-hemolytic streptococci (the bacteria that causes strep throat) and Tourette's and OCD. In 1996, Susan Swedo, the acting scientific director at the National Institute of Mental Health, released a statement encouraging parents to get a throat culture for any child who presents "acute onset or exacerbation of obsessive-compulsive or tic symptoms." Her statement goes on to say "Our studies and others on obsessive-compulsive disorder are truly proof that these are neurobiological illnesses, that what was previously thought to be due to punitive toilet training is now known to be associated with changes in brain chemicals and patterns of responsiveness of glucose metabolism, and now, perhaps, triggered by an autoimmune reaction." A study at Johns Hopkins corroborated these findings and determined that "some children with Tourette's syndrome had higher levels of the antibodies that the body creates to fight strep infection than did children without Tourette's." Harvey Singer, the head of pediatric neurology at Hopkins, explains, "The theory is that the body makes antibodies against strep that react against cells in the brain." Apparently, the antibodies that attack strep also attack an area of the brain called the putamen, which helps control movement and is thought to be involved in Tourette's and related disorders.

What this means is that in susceptible children—and susceptible is the key word here; none of this bears any relevance on those not genetically predisposed to the disorders—a strep infection can trigger an autoimmune response in the body that can lead to symptoms, or a full-blown version, of Tourette's or OCD. When children with Tourette's or OCD associated with streptococcal infections were treated with penicillin, they improved dramatically.

I suffered from several severe bouts of strep throat when I was very young, as did Bryant, it turns out. When I was just months old I almost died when an ear infection was treated, as per the norm, with penicillin, and I experienced an allergic reaction to the drug that was almost more than my body could tolerate; I was interested to note that Bryant, too, had been found to be allergic to penicillin at a young age and had not been treated with it since. We are two individuals in what is still a vast and murky sea of research and unique experiences, but such detective work leads me closer, baby step by baby step, to understanding both my own condition and these mystifying disorders in general. I beseech parents and all those with symptoms that strike them or those around them as suspicious or troubling to seek professional evaluation sooner rather than later: Self-awareness is the first and, in the end, the very best treatment of all.

The Tourette Syndrome Association
42-40 Bell Boulevard
Bayside, NY 11361-2820
Tel.: (718) 224-2999
Fax: (718) 279-9596
e-mail: tourette@ix.netcom.com

The Obsessive-Compulsive Foundation
P.O. Box 70
Milford, CT 06460-0070
Tel.: (203) 878-5669
Fax: (203) 874-2826

Amy S. Wilensky is a graduate of Vassar College and Columbia University's M.F.A. writing program. A native of suburban Boston, she lives in New York City.

Printed in the United States
by Baker & Taylor Publisher Services